The Institute of Chartered Financial Analysts Continuing Education Series

Managing Currency Risk

June 22, 1989
Boston, Massachusetts

Fischer Black
Richard C. Carr, CFA
Dean D'Onofrio, CFA
Mark P. Kritzman, CFA
Adrian F. Lee
Mack Ott
Carol W. Proffer
James E. Rhodes, CFA
Michael R. Rosenberg

Edited by
Mark P. Kritzman, CFA and Katrina F. Sherrerd

Sponsored by
The Institute of Chartered
Financial Analysts

Additional copies of this publication may be ordered from

Institute of Chartered Financial Analysts
P.O. Box 3668
Charlottesville, VA 22903
1-804-980-3647

Katrina F. Sherrerd, *Managing Editor*
Joni L. Tomal, *Editorial Assistant*
Diane B. Hamshar, *Administrative Assistant*

ISBN 0-935015-15-9

Printed in the United States of America

Table of Contents

Foreword

International investing is growing rapidly among institutional and individual investors. The benefits and risks of international investment are attracting considerable attention in the financial press—both academic and practitioner. Everyone is trying to ascertain the best way to reap the benefits of diversification and manage the risks associated with international investing.

The multi-currency dimension of international investing is one of the critical areas for portfolio managers. There is substantial risk embedded in the currency exposure of foreign investment, but it is not clear how investors should manage that risk. The question of whether to hedge currency exposure, and if so, how much to hedge, are just two of the many questions facing investors seeking international exposure.

As readers will learn in these proceedings, there is not a simple solution to the question of whether to hedge and how much to hedge. Some portfolio managers treat hedging vehicles as a separate asset class that should be managed to add incremental return, and others view hedging as risk that must be diversified away at the expense of having a negative effect on portfolio returns.

As institutions increase their investments in foreign markets, knowledge of currency management becomes imperative. The issues surrounding managing currency risk were addressed at a seminar sponsored by the ICFA on June 22, 1989. This program was organized by Darwin M. Bayston, CFA, Executive Vice President, and Susan D. Martin, Vice President—Education and Programs at the Institute of Chartered Financial Analysts. This publication is the result of that seminar.

This is the third time the Institute has addressed the subject of international investing in this Continuing Education Series of seminars and proceedings. The first was *International Equity Investing,* published in 1984, and the second was *International Bonds and Currencies,* published in 1986. Separately or in combination, these three publications offer an important resource on the issues facing portfolio managers involved with international investing.

The perspectives of leading professionals in the international market were expressed at this seminar. Their expertise on this subject makes these proceedings a valuable contribution to the literature on international investing. The ICFA wishes to extend its sincere appreciation to the seminar speakers: Fischer Black, Goldman, Sachs & Co.; Richard Carr, First Chicago Investment Advisors; Dean D'Onofrio, Bankers Trust Company; Mark Kritzman, Windham Capital Management; Adrian Lee, J.P. Morgan Investment Management; Mack Ott, Federal Reserve Bank of St. Louis; Carol Proffer, Mercer Meidinger Hansen; James Rhodes, Bechtel Investments; and Michael Rosenberg, Merrill Lynch Capital Markets.

Special thanks to Robert J. Schwob of Citibank, who acted as moderator at the seminar, and to Mark Kritzman for co-editing the proceedings.

Katrina F. Sherrerd
Assistant Vice President
Research and Publications

Biographies of Speakers

Fischer Black is a Partner in the Trading and Arbitrage Division of Goldman, Sachs & Co. He works to apply analytical methods to the firm's business, for its own investments and for its clients. Before joining Goldman Sachs, he was professor of finance at MIT's Sloan School of Management and at the University of Chicago. Dr. Black developed, with Myron Scholes, the Black-Scholes option pricing formula. Dr. Black holds an A.B. in physics from Harvard University and a Ph.D. in applied mathematics from Harvard University.

Richard C. Carr, CFA is Managing Director and Division Head of the International Division of First Chicago Investment Advisors. Mr. Carr joined First Chicago Corporation in 1964 as a Research Analyst in the Investment Research Division. He is a member of the Financial Analysts Federation, the Investment Analysts Society of Chicago, the London Society of Investment Analysts, and the Chicago Council on Foreign Relations. Mr. Carr co-authored an article in the *Financial Analysts Journal* (July/August, 1982) for which he received the Graham and Dodd Scroll Award for Excellence. He holds a B.A. from Yale University and an M.B.A. from Northwestern University.

Dean D'Onofrio, CFA is Vice President, Global Quantitative Strategies, of the Investment Management Group of Bankers Trust Company. In this position, he directs the unit responsible for research, development and management of quantitative investment strategies worldwide. Mr. D'Onofrio holds degrees in mathematics and economics and has eight years of investment experience at Bankers Trust.

Mark P. Kritzman, CFA is a founding Partner of Windham Capital Management. Previously, he was a general partner of New Amsterdam Partners, a vice president of Bankers Trust Company, and held investment positions at AT&T and The Equitable Life Assurance Society. Mr. Kritzman is a member of the Candidate Curriculum Committee of the ICFA and a member of the Review Board of the Institute's Research Foundation. He has published numerous articles and contributed several chapters on the application of financial theory to investment management, and is co-editor and co-author with S.J. Brown of *Quantitative Methods for Financial Analysis* (Dow Jones-Irwin). Mr. Kritzman holds a B.S. degree from St. John's University and an M.B.A. from New York University.

Adrian F. Lee is a Vice President at J.P. Morgan Investment Management, Inc., responsible for international capital markets research and new product development. Prior to joining Morgan in 1980, Mr. Lee worked at Winklevoss and Associates in Philadelphia and at the University of Pennsylvania as a lecturer in statistics. Mr. Lee joined the International Investment Group in London in 1984. He is the author of several publications on global asset allocation and currency hedging. Mr. Lee holds an M.A. in mathematical economics and statistics from Trinity College Dublin and an M.B.A. in finance and actuarial science from the Wharton School of the University of Pennsylvania.

Mack Ott joined the Research Department at the Federal Reserve Bank of St. Louis in 1981. Prior to that, he was on the economics faculties at Virginia Polytechnic Institute and State University and Pennsylvania State University. He has been a visiting scholar at the Federal Reserve Bank of St. Louis and a visiting professor of monetary economics at Erasmus University Rotterdam. Dr. Ott has published widely on topics in monetary and macroeconomic theory, energy economics, the economics of bureaucracy and international finance. His current research is focused on the determinants of exchange rates and the macroeconomics of the open economy. Dr. Ott holds a Ph.D. from the University of California at Los Angeles.

Carol W. Proffer is a Managing Director of William M. Mercer Meidinger Hansen, Inc. responsible for the company's southwest region asset planning practice. She has taught seminars and sessions for the Society of Actuaries in Public Practice, addressed investment-related sessions concerning pension plan expensing and portfolio insurance, and testified for the Department of Labor on the analysis of the appropriateness of whole life insurance products as an investment vehicle for severance payment plans. She is a member of the Pension Committee of the IASB, American Academy of Actuaries and a Fellow of the Society of Actuaries. Ms. Proffer holds a B.S. degree from Milligan College and an M.S. from

Oklahoma State University.

James E. Rhodes, CFA is a Principal with Bechtel Investments, Inc. (BII) and Senior Vice President of Sierra Asset Management, Inc., a subsidiary of BII. Mr. Rhodes is Chairman of the firm's asset allocation committee and is responsible for strategies related to U.S. and non-U.S. equity managers, tactical asset allocation managers, and long-range investment planning for the fund. He is also Director and Senior Vice President of Fremont Mutual Funds, Inc. The author of several articles, Mr. Rhodes holds an M.B.A. from the University of California at Berkeley.

Michael R. Rosenberg is Manager of the International Fixed Income Research Department at Merrill Lynch Capital Markets, which publishes a weekly review of global bond market and currency trends, a bi-weekly review of yield curve and yield spread developments in all major bond markets, a monthly international economic and financial calendar, a monthly review on global liability management, a quarterly review on global bond portfolio strategy, and monthly reviews on several foreign bond markets. Prior to joining Merrill Lynch, he worked as director of international bond management for Prudential Insurance Company of America; an international economist for Chase Manhattan Bank; and a senior currency and international money market analyst for Citibank. Dr. Rosenberg holds a B.S. in accounting from the State University of New York in Albany, an M.A. in economics from Queens College, and a Ph.D. in economics from Penn State University.

Overview of the Seminar

Mark P. Kritzman, CFA

After almost 30 years of fixed exchange rates following the Bretton Woods Agreement in 1944, the international monetary system progressively evolved toward a system of floating exchange rates. Several countries began to experiment with floating exchange rates in 1973. In 1976, the major trading partners formally agreed to a system of floating exchange rates. Since then, the long-term average return of most major currencies has not been significantly different from zero, but the year-to-year volatility has averaged approximately 10 percent.

At the same time, investors are becoming increasingly global in their perspective. Portfolio managers are investing internationally. Because of the increased exposure of institutional portfolios to foreign investment, portfolio managers must address the issue of the risk emanating from the embedded currency exposure of foreign investment. To address the important issues surrounding managing currency risk, the Institute of Chartered Financial Analysts held a seminar on this topic. The speakers addressed such issues as the merits and methods of currency hedging, currency management strategies to add value, and execution of currency strategies using derivative instruments. These proceedings are the result of that seminar.

A casual reading of these proceedings may suggest that the speakers disagree sharply on some of the important issues regarding currency management—in particular, the decision of whether to hedge currency exposure. As we will attempt to demonstrate in the summary, however, this ostensible divergence of opinion can be reconciled, for the most part, by consideration of the speakers' assumptions and perspectives.

TO HEDGE OR NOT TO HEDGE?

James Rhodes and Carol Proffer directly address the question of whether currency hedging is appropriate. In the first part of the session, Rhodes argues that the decision to hedge depends on a fund's allocation to foreign investments and the desire to protect retirement benefits from inflation. His empirical research shows that by hedging the currency exposure of foreign investments, allocating a greater percentage of the fund to foreign investments increases a portfolio's expected return without increasing its risk.

Rhodes argues that typically there is no significant benefit from hedging if a fund's allocation to foreign investments is less than 10 percent. As the allocation grows, however, it is typically optimal to hedge some fraction of the currency exposure.

Rhodes advocates a protective put option strategy as an effective way to control currency risk. This strategy, which is a special case of the dynamic hedging approach described by Proffer, limits negative returns from currency exposure while capturing some fraction of the gains that may result from currency exposure.

In the second part of the session, Proffer addresses the broad issues underlying the decision on whether to hedge. She cites two motivations for the growing interest in currency hedging: (1) the risk that the dollar may strengthen and thereby reduce the unrealized gains that U.S. investors have achieved during the past few years in the foreign capital markets, and (2) the realization that currency-hedged portfolios typically exhibit less risk for a given level of return than unhedged portfolios.

Proffer describes three approaches to currency hedging: (1) a passive approach in which a portfolio is hedged fully and continually in the forward market, (2) a dynamic approach in which the hedge ratio is determined in such a way as to limit downside risk from currency exposure, and (3) active hedging whereby the timing and the degree of currency hedging depends on one's outlook for currency returns. Proffer points out that hedging can be executed "in house" by the fund sponsor, by the manager of the underlying foreign investments, or by an overlay manager who may specialize in currency hedging.

HEDGING DECISIONS WITHIN THE OVERALL ASSET ALLOCATION STRATEGY

Adrian Lee discusses hedging decisions within the overall asset allocation strategy. He recommends that the asset allocation process should be partitioned into three decisions: the decision between domestic and international assets, the decision between international stocks and bonds, and the decision between international assets and currencies. He points out that a foreign asset's return has two components: the local return and the currency return. He introduces the notion of a "pure" foreign asset for which the currency exposure has been fully hedged.

Based on empirical studies, Lee claims that the risk-reduction benefit from hedging is about equal to the risk reduction that would occur by switching from a stock portfolio to a bond portfolio. Moreover, Lee argues that the improvement in a portfolio's risk-return trade-off that results from hedging is at least as great as the improvement that results from international diversification. Because, over the long run, a hedged portfolio should not outperform an unhedged portfolio, Lee advocates hedging a fund's currency exposure fully as a normal policy. Not to hedge, he argues, implies the expectation that the currency's return will exceed the forward premium.

UNIVERSAL HEDGING

Fischer Black develops an equilibrium theory of currency hedging which contains some rather unintuitive results and prescriptions. Based on a set of assumptions that might be considered restrictive, Black concludes that all investors, regardless of the country in which they are domiciled, should hedge the same amount of their currency exposure. Moreover, the amount to hedge does not depend on the currencies' expected returns, nor on their correlations with each other and other assets. Finally, Black demonstrates that currency transactions are not zero-sum events. These transactions are positive-sum events because of Siegel's paradox. For equities, this results in an optimal universal hedge ratio of less than 100 percent. A corollary of Black's insight is that simply by the force of mathematics, the forward exchange rate cannot be an unbiased estimate of the future spot rate for both sides of the transaction, because the percentage change implied by the forward rates differs for the two parties. Thus, if the forward rate is an unbiased estimate of the future spot rate for one side of the transaction, it necessarily must be biased for the other side of the transaction.

MEASURING THE EFFECTIVENESS OF CURRENCY HEDGING STRATEGIES

Richard Carr approaches the currency hedging issue from the perspective of a policy decision rather than a strategic or tactical asset allocation decision. Carr views the resultant reduction in risk as the primary motivation for currency hedging. He points out, however, that there is a trade-off between loss of diversification and lower volatility, which on balance favors currency hedging. Carr also considers the impact of currency hedging when liabilities are included, because unhedged foreign assets are more highly correlated with liabilities than are hedged foreign assets. Finally, Carr demonstrates that the description of a normal portfolio will depend on whether currency exposure is hedged. The normal portfolio will tend to include a higher percentage of foreign assets if the embedded currency exposure is hedged because hedged foreign assets are less risky than unhedged foreign assets.

HEDGING OPPORTUNITIES

Mark Kritzman discusses hedging as both a defensive strategy and a strategy for adding value to a fund. As a defensive strategy, he presents an algorithm for minimizing portfolio risk. He shows that by estimating currency returns as the percentage change in moving from the forward exchange rate at the beginning of the period to the spot rate at the end of the period, the dynamics of the interest differential are subsumed in the parameter estimates, which results in a much simpler hedging algorithm.

Kritzman also argues that investors can generate profits by varying a fund's exposure to currencies in accordance with a particular class of linear investment rules. According to Kritzman, central banks intervene regularly in the currency market to cushion exchange rates when they are exposed to disturbances. This intervention induces significant non-randomness in dollar-denominated currency returns, which he confirms by both parametric and non-parametric statistical tests. Investors can exploit non-randomness in currency returns by following investment strategies that generate convex payoff functions. Kritzman demonstrates that the timing skill embedded in these convex strategies is statistically significant at a confidence level exceeding 99 percent. Moreover, a conservative convex strategy diversified across the five major currencies has added value in 10 of the past 12 years.

EVALUATING CURRENCIES AS A SEPARATE ASSET CLASS

Mack Ott argues that forward exchange rates encompass a risk premium as compensation for accepting a risky outcome. The existence of a risk premium requires either periodic or systematic departures from purchasing power parity. Ott cites several references which provide empirical confirmation of a risk premium. He suggests that if indeed central banks resist long-term movements in exchange rates, investors may profit by betting against the central banks, provided their horizon is longer than the central banks' horizon. This notion is consistent with Kritzman's evidence of non-randomness in currency returns.

HEDGING A NON-DOLLAR FIXED-INCOME PORTFOLIO

Michael Rosenberg disputes the notion that currency hedging provides a free lunch for bond portfolios, as advanced by Perold and Schulman in a recent *Financial Analysts Journal* article. Perold and Schulman (1988) argued that currency hedging reduces risk without reducing expected return. Rosenberg disagrees because he believes that over the long run, the greater diversification benefits of an unhedged bond portfolio offset the lower volatility benefits of a hedged portfolio. He argues further that the costs associated with currency hedging lower a hedged portfolio's expected return. He concludes that investors should invest internationally, not to reduce risk, but to add value through active management of both the underlying assets and the currency exposure.

EXECUTING CURRENCY HEDGING STRATEGIES

Dean D'Onofrio reviews the various approaches for executing currency strategies, including the use of futures contracts, forward contracts, and currency options. D'Onofrio points out that currency forward markets are the most liquid in the world, with daily volume far surpassing the volume on the New York Stock Exchange. He distinguishes futures from forward contracts. Futures contracts have uniform terms with respect to quantity, maturity, and underlying asset, resulting in a vast secondary market. These contracts require margin deposits. For small positions, futures contracts may be less expensive to trade than forward contracts. Forward contracts are negotiated privately between the buyer and seller, and thus are usually held to maturity. They do not typically require margin deposits. For large positions, forward contracts are typically less expensive to trade.

SUMMARY

Several contradictions seem apparent from the comments of the speakers. Most of the speakers argue that currency hedging usually benefits an internationally diversified portfolio, although the optimal hedge ratio may not always equal 100 percent and would typically vary across investors. Black, however, advocates that all investors should hedge their currency exposure by the same amount, while Rosenberg claims that hedging any amount of currency exposure as a general policy is counterproductive.

These seemingly contradictory views can be reconciled by noting that the speakers base their analyses on different assumptions. Black's assertion depends on several assumptions—in particular, the assumption that all investors hold the same underlying portfolio, which is the world market portfolio. It is this assumption that gives rise to a universal constant for hedging currency exposure. The critical assumption underlying Rosenberg's conclusion that currency hedging is counterproductive is that investors have 10- to 16-year investment horizons. Because hedging costs increase linearly with time while risk increases with the square root of time, it is easy to see why currency hedging may not yield benefits over extremely long investment horizons. However, if we reject the assumption that all investors hold the world market portfolio and that performance over one-, two-, or five-year periods is important, the consensus is that currency hedging is generally beneficial, and that the appropriate hedge ratio is, in part, a function of considerations that are unique to each investor.

The speakers also seem to disagree on the costs associated with currency hedging, with estimates ranging from 10 to 70 basis points. Again, these apparent contradictions may be reconciled by examining some of the underlying assumptions. Some of the speakers referred to strategies for which the optimal hedge ratio was significantly less than 100 percent of the embedded currency exposure and revisions occurred infrequently. Other speakers referred to strategies in which 100 percent of the currency exposure was hedged continually, requiring monthly rebalancing. It is easy to see how these distinctions can result in significantly different estimates of hedging costs.

Perhaps the most important message in these proceedings is that currency management is an important and distinct investment activity. Moreover, as international diversification grows, so will the importance of currency management and the sophistication brought to bear on the issue.

To Hedge or Not to Hedge? (Part I)

James E. Rhodes, CFA

Currency risk hedging is either a useful management tool or a non-issue for most retirement plans. The answer depends on the plan's perceived need to control risk and its allocation to and its commitment to international diversification. Furthermore, recent studies have suggested that a normal currency hedge policy should be influenced by the overall foreign allocation and the desire to maintain an inflation hedge in retirement fund assets. Once the normal policy is established, a plan may choose to adjust its currency exposure on the basis of a tactical view regarding the outlook for currency values; or a plan may consider implementing a protective put option strategy. With the option approach, losses should be limited during strong dollar periods and gains should occur during weak dollar periods. In the past year, considerable debate has focused on whether retirement funds should hedge the currency exposure of their foreign allocation.

In this presentation I will provide a brief review of historical relationships of risk, return, and correlation statistics for foreign assets, with and without currency hedging. Second, I will take a look at portfolio diversification in an *ex ante*, or forward-looking, context. Third, I will look at the issue of maintaining the purchasing power of retirement plan assets while setting a normal policy for currency hedging. Finally, I will discuss some tactical currency exposure tactics, contrasting traditional approaches with protective put option strategies.

BECHTEL'S EVALUATION OF CURRENCY RISK

The Bechtel retirement plan's allocation to the foreign area exceeded 20 percent in late 1986. Foreign exchange risk was perceived as a key risk factor in our overall risk of managing the portfolio. Although currency exposure was contributing positively to fund results at that time, the staff began to evaluate how currency risk affects portfolio diversification and how a strong dollar could negatively impact fund results. The evaluation concentrated on the risk and return characteristics of unhedged and hedged foreign assets and how to control currency risk from both the normal policy and tactical strategy standpoint. The staff enlisted support from Wells Fargo Investment Advisors and J. P. Morgan. These managers were extremely cooperative in providing data and suggestions regarding possible normal policy and tactical strategy approaches.

Table 1 presents a summary of the historical statistics of domestic and foreign assets on an unhedged and hedged basis for the 10 years ending December 1987. It is unlikely that the long-term implications for risk and correlation relationships will be materially affected if the 1988 results are included, or if a longer period is evaluated. Based on the data in Table 1, the following conclusions can be made about the long-term relationships.

- First, currency hedging can reduce foreign equity risk (i.e., standard deviation) by 20 to 25 percent, bringing the riskiness of foreign equity assets more in line with the domestic equity risk.
- Second, hedging reduces foreign bond risk even more substantially—by about 50 to 60 percent. The hedging of foreign bonds reduces the risk level to that of domestic intermediate bonds. On an unhedged basis, foreign bonds have a risk level similar to domestic long bonds. As a result, plan sponsors who constrain the exposure to long bonds in their portfolio may prefer hedged or partially hedged foreign bonds over unhedged foreign bonds.
- Third, the correlation between domestic assets and foreign assets increases somewhat when foreign exchange risk is hedged. Hence, the elimination of currency risk reduces the diversification benefit between these assets.
- Fourth, the correlation between foreign stocks and foreign bonds decreases when these assets are hedged. For this period, the correlation falls to 0.20 from 0.56. This can be an important diversification element when a significant portion of a portfolio is allocated to hedged foreign equities and hedged foreign bonds.

Clearly, hedging currency risk modifies the characteristics of foreign assets, but for the most part, these changes improve the desirability of these assets from the standpoint of portfolio diversification.

TABLE 1. Historical Statistics (1978-1987)

Indexes	*Return*	*Risk*	*Correlations* 1	2	3	4	5	6
U.S. equity	15.2%	17.2%	1.00					
Foreign equity unhedged	22.8%	19.1%	0.63	1.00				
Foreign equity hedged	21.3%	14.0%	0.63	0.77	1.00			
U.S. bonds	10.3%	10.1%	0.31	0.33	0.17	1.00		
Foreign bonds unhedged	13.4%	16.3%	0.17	0.56	0.04	0.58	1.00	
Foreign bonds hedged	11.2%	6.7%	0.18	0.33	0.20	0.73	0.67	1.00

Legend	*Index*
U.S. equity	S&P 500 Index
Foreign equity	Morgan Stanley EAFE Index
U.S. bonds	Shearson Lehman Government/Corporate Bond Index
Foreign bonds	Salomon Brothers Non-Dollar Index
Source of hedged returns	J.P. Morgan Investment Management

Source: Bechtel Investments, Inc.

A "FORWARD-LOOKING" VIEW OF HEDGED FOREIGN ASSETS

Table 2 shows the risk, return, and asset mix assumptions used in this portfolio diversification analysis. The expected risk and correlation data are assumed to be similar to the historical statistics. Within an asset category, the expected return forecasts are the same regardless of whether the asset is domestic or foreign, hedged or unhedged. The expected return estimate for equity is based on a recent dividend discount model forecast, and the expected return for bonds is based on the recent yield-to-maturity.

The parity of domestic and foreign assets eliminates expected return bias from the analysis and focuses attention primarily on the issue of portfolio diversification. Table 2 shows the effect on portfolio diversification when foreign assets are brought into a domestic-only portfolio of 60 percent equity and 40 percent bonds. The domestic-only portfolio (Mix #1) has an estimated risk level of 12.1 percent. Mix #2 shows the allocation of 10 percent to unhedged foreign equity and 5 percent to unhedged foreign bonds. This mix reduces the portfolio risk to 11.8 percent. An allocation of 20 percent to unhedged foreign equity and 10 percent to unhedged foreign bonds does not further diversify the portfolio; in fact, the portfolio risk level increases slightly to 11.9 percent. This result is in sharp contrast to portfolio risk levels associated with hedged foreign asset diversification.

A portfolio that includes hedged foreign assets—10 percent equity and 5 percent bonds—has an estimated risk level of 11.2 percent, much lower than the unhedged portfolios. When the allocation is doubled to 20 percent foreign equity and 10 percent hedged foreign bonds, the risk level falls to 10.4 percent. Shifting another 5 percent increment to both hedged foreign equity and bonds reduces the portfolio risk level to 10.1 percent. This demonstrates that in the long run, by hedging currency risk, portfolio risk is reduced and a higher foreign

TABLE 2. Portfolio Diversification Assumptions

	Expected Return (%)	*Expected Risk (%)*	*Portfolio Mix (%)* 1	2	3	4	5	6	7
U.S equity	12.0	17.0	60	50	40	50	40	35	40
Foreign equity unhedged	12.0	19.0		10	20				
Foreign equity hedged	12.0	14.0				10	20	25	25
U.S. bonds	8.9	10.0	40	35	30	35	30	25	20
Foreign bonds unhedged	8.9	16.0		5	10				
Foreign bonds hedged	8.9	7.0				5	10	15	15
		Portfolio Risk	12.1	11.8	11.9	11.2	10.4	10.1	10.6
		Portfolio Return	10.8	10.8	10.8	10.8	10.8	10.8	10.9

Source: Bechtel Investments, Inc.

allocation is appropriate, from an optimal portfolio standpoint.

An additional benefit from hedging currency risk is that more of the portfolio can be allocated to the equity asset category without increasing risk. Mix #7 shows that when an extra 5 percent is allocated to domestic equity from domestic bonds, the resulting portfolio has a higher expected return than all of the other mixes and a lower risk level than all of the unhedged mixes.

As retirement plans diversify internationally, the evidence is clear that maximum diversification benefit can be achieved by integrating currency hedge policies with asset allocation policies. This can be done in a framework that accommodates both long-term or normal asset allocation policies and short-term or tactical strategies. Unless a plan considers its exposure to future obligations, this analysis suggests that a 100 percent hedge should be the normal currency hedge policy. There are reasons, however, why a 100 percent currency hedge policy should not be the normal currency hedge policy for most retirement plans.

SETTING A NORMAL CURRENCY HEDGE POLICY

Recently, it has been argued that there should be some normal currency exposure to hedge against a loss of purchasing power due to imported inflation. For domestic plans, future obligations can be thought of as a set of future consumption baskets for plan participants. Because imported goods and services represent a substantial portion of overall consumption, a weak dollar's negative impact on inflation can be hedged by maintaining some normal currency exposure. Recent studies suggest that one way to estimate an appropriate exposure level for plan assets is to measure the percentage of imports to GNP. Currently, this relationship is around 10 percent for the United States.

If this percentage is to represent the net overall exposure, normal currency hedge policies should vary according to a plan's commitment to foreign assets. The more a fund has allocated to foreign assets, the greater is the portion of currency risk that should be hedged. For example, a fund with only a 10 percent allocation to foreign assets may not want to hedge currency risk in a normal policy sense. On the other hand, a fund with a 30 percent foreign allocation may want to assign a normal currency hedge that is about two-thirds of the allocation, thus maintaining an overall 10 percent exposure to currency risk in a policy sense. Some large funds are beginning to exceed an overall 30 percent allocation, suggesting that an even greater normal hedge policy target may be appropriate. In the absence of a tactical currency view, a plan would want to maintain its currency exposure in line with the normal policy.

TACTICAL CURRENCY EXPOSURE

There are several approaches to implementing tactical currency exposure. I will discuss three: active management with restatement of benchmarks, overlay strategies, and protective put strategies. If a plan sponsor is only interested in maintaining its normal currency exposure, rolling one-month or three-month forward contracts is an effective way to implement the desired hedge policy. This constant hedge approach is an inexpensive way to implement the desired hedge policy on either a full or partial basis. It is simple to calculate and implement, requiring no rebalancing until the contracts are rolled forward.

Other sponsors may want to integrate tactical strategies with the setting of their normal currency policy. One way is to restate individual manager performance benchmarks to include the normal currency policy of the plan sponsor. In this way, the manager will develop active currency strategies relative to the sponsor's normal policy. For example, when the manager has a neutral outlook, the currency exposure should be similar to the exposure of the restated benchmark.

Another approach is to use an overlay strategy that incorporates underlying individual manager currency positions into one net currency position relative to the sponsor's normal policy. This can be implemented either on an active or a constant hedge basis.

Third, one can use protective put option strategies. A protective put strategy will limit negative returns to a prescribed floor when the dollar is strong and allow upside participation when the dollar is weak. This strategy offers the plan sponsor a way to control currency exposure from both the tactical strategy and normal policy standpoint. This can be done by varying option policy floors relative to a plan's normal currency hedge policy.

Figures 1 and 2 illustrate the return trade-offs for two normal constant hedge policies with two alternative protective put strategies. These graphs reflect the market conditions in the spring of 1989. As shown in **Figure 1**, a plan with a 50 percent normal currency hedge policy could incorporate a tactical strategy by employing a one-year, -5 percent floor put option strategy. The option strategy would do better when currency returns are above +8 percent or below -12 percent. Within this range, the 50 percent partial hedge does better. **Figure 2** shows that a plan with a 75 percent normal currency hedge

FIGURE 1. Fifty Percent Partial Hedge Versus Negative Five Percent Floor Option

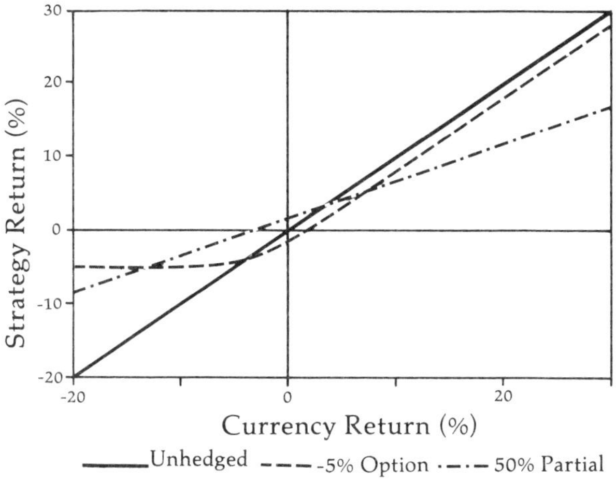

Source: Bechtel Investments, Inc.

FIGURE 2. Seventy-five Percent Partial Hedge Versus Zero Percent Floor Option

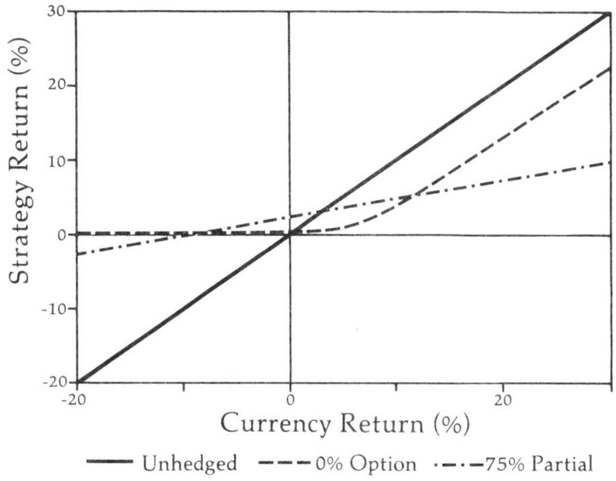

Source: Bechtel Investments, Inc.

policy could consider a zero percent floor put option strategy as an alternative. Here the option strategy does better when the currency returns are above 12 percent or below -10 percent. Otherwise, the partial hedge is the preferred strategy.

The manager of our passive foreign assets has been managing currency option strategies for us since the fourth quarter of 1987. This is being done dynamically, using the Chicago Mercantile currency futures markets. The approach hedges a basket of currencies that is a proxy for our passive equity and bond portfolio currency exposures. Although the strategy could be applied using individual currency options, the currency basket approach is more efficient because an option on a portfolio is less costly than a portfolio of options.

Table 3 shows the results of historical currency hedge simulations conducted for the 11-year period ending 1988. Two one-year policies are shown. The first column shows that on an unhedged basis, the currency return was 3.6 percent over the 11-year period, with considerable year-to-year volatility, ranging from -12.1 percent in 1981 to 28.4 percent in 1987. The -5 percent floor option strategy outperformed the 50 percent partial hedge alternative, with returns of 5.1 percent versus 3.6 percent, respectively. The zero percent floor option strategy outperformed the 75 percent partial hedge strategy, with returns of 5.2 percent versus 3.5 percent, respectively. Although year-to-year return volatility is greater for the option strategies than for the partial hedge policies, in most years the different returns are related to better performance. In years when the dollar was strong, the option strategies avoided much of the associated negative returns. In years when the dollar was weak, substantial upside participation occurred.

Table 4 shows the performance results of our existing currency option policies. Foreign bonds have been assigned a more conservative option policy to create an asset that is similar in risk to our domestic bond portfolio. Bechtel's domestic bond portfolio is closer to intermediate bond risk than to long bond risk. Currently, the dynamic nature of the option strategies has both accounts fully hedged against currency exposure. Assuming the dollar stays firm, account results are on target to meet the prescribed floor returns by the end of the policy period.

TABLE 3. Currency Hedge Simulation (In EAFE Weights)

	Foreign Exchange Return	*75% Partial Hedge*	*vs.*	*0% Floor Option Return*	*50% Partial Hedge*	*vs.*	*-5% Floor Option Return*
1988	-1.2%	1.7%		0.2%	0.8%		-2.2%
1987	28.4	8.7		17.9	15.3		25.5
1986	20.2	5.8		7.9	10.6		16.2
1985	26.3	7.3		14.8	13.6		23.7
1984	-11.9	-0.0		1.9	-4.0		-3.2
1983	-6.4	0.3		0.6	-2.0		-3.9
1982	-8.5	1.0		2.3	-2.2		-2.7
1981	-12.1	2.0		4.7	-2.7		-0.4
1980	2.1	2.1		0.5	2.1		-1.2
1979	-3.3	2.2		2.1	0.3		-2.1
1978	17.3	7.5		5.8	10.8		12.8
Annualized Return	3.6	3.5		5.2	3.6		5.1

Source: Wells Fargo Investment Advisors and Bechtel Investments, Inc.

TABLE 4. Performance of Existing Currency Option Policies

	Foreign Equity Currency Hedge	*Foreign Bonds Currency Hedge*
Option Policy	-5.0% Floor	0% Floor
Policy Horizon	13 Months Ending 12/89	12 Months Ending 12/89
	6 Months Ending May 1989	*5 Months Ending May 1989*
Currency Basket	-14.2%	-11.1%
Hedge Return	- 5.6%	- 1.1%
Difference	8.6%	10.0%

Source: Bechtel Investments, Inc.

CONCLUSION

Several conclusions can be drawn from this presentation. First, hedging currency risk is beneficial, but the degree is a function of a plan's normal policies, tactical strategies, and the overall foreign allocation. Second, from an inflation hedge standpoint, some foreign currency exposure appears appropriate. Third, plans with substantial foreign assets should hedge a greater portion of the currency risk than plans with fewer foreign assets. Fourth, depending on the current environment, a tactical deviation from the normal policy may be appropriate and can be implemented in a number of ways. Finally, the use of currency option strategies may be an attractive way for plan sponsors to control currency risk exposure while participating in currency gains when the dollar is weak.

To Hedge or Not to Hedge? (Part II)

Carol W. Proffer

To hedge or not to hedge? That is a question plan sponsors must address. In this presentation, I will discuss some of the key issues plan sponsors must consider in analyzing currency hedging and how it might fit into the overall management of their portfolios.

WHY CONSIDER HEDGING?

There are several reasons why plan sponsors should consider hedging. First, the world market has experienced attractive returns over the past eight or nine years. A major reason for this good performance is the softening of the dollar. Plan sponsors do not want to give up these returns, so protecting against a strengthened dollar becomes an issue.

Second, currency volatility exists. Increased participation in worldwide investing has generated more interest in what creates the return and also what creates fluctuations in returns. Hedging may be used to manage volatility.

Third, some recent research has produced results that are contrary to the previously accepted philosophical positions on currency hedging. The idea that a hedged portfolio might produce lower volatility at the same level of expected return than an unhedged portfolio is a bit contrary to what many people have believed.

The types of international investing pursued affect the currency approaches to be considered. For example, currency is not factored into the decision process for indexed international equity funds. The currency component is the same as the component that identifies the benchmark or the index; there is no specific, distinct decision made with respect to currency positions. Second, if a portfolio is based on world market capitalization, there would be a heavy exposure to the Japanese yen. In this case, one might want to encourage plan sponsors to think about some type of currency hedging. Third, in a globalized economy, issues such as flow of funds, trade balances, and other factors that are becoming more and more apparent to U.S. investors are having a greater impact on currency decisions.

Active international investors have additional reasons for looking at hedging. First, they are concerned about how the question of hedging is being addressed. They recognize that currency is factored into the investment decision-making process, but is this sufficient? Is the currency issue being looked at the way the sponsor wants it to be addressed? Second, there is concern about duplication of efforts. As plan sponsors add more complementary styles of investing outside the United States, they do not want their currency management to offset or negate other actions. There is also concern about overexposure to one currency.

Currency is a major factor on the fixed-income side. Currency decisions equal about 50 percent of the fixed-income investment process, and consequently, currency issues are of even greater concern than for equity portfolios. Over the past several years, interest in investing in global fixed-income has risen. If a plan sponsor has a predisposition as to the amount of exposure to each currency bloc, some type of hedging should be considered.

Another major reason that currency must be addressed by plan sponsors is the fact that, ultimately, benefits must be paid in U.S. dollars. The issue of hedging relates to when the conversion occurs. Does it need to occur earlier, through some type of hedging process, or later? The hedging decision is affected by the investor's investment horizon and when the dollars need to be converted back to the base currency.

Performance expectations are another reason that hedging is of interest. In light of recent analysis of the returns produced and the factors that have created those returns, there may be some unrealistic expectations.

APPROACHES TO HEDGING

There are three basic approaches to hedging: passive, dynamic, and active. In passive hedging, there is continuous conversion, by the use of forward contracts, back to the U.S. dollar (or back to the base currency if the funds are non-U.S.). This approach removes all explicit multi-currency exposure, because everything is being moved back into U.S. dollars. One cannot, however, remove the implicit exposure to stock prices—that is, the changes in a country and, in turn, the changes in the currency that implicitly affect local stock prices.

Dynamic hedging can be thought of as portfolio

insurance on currency. This approach involves setting a minimum level of exposure for downside participation in currency fluctuations, and using options or futures to limit the downside exposure—but allowing participation in upside movements in the currency relationships. This approach assumes there is a desire to partially participate in the currency movements, but limit losses caused by adverse currency movements.

Active hedging describes the situation where one is attempting to add value (or return) with currencies, or alternatively, to control risk through managing currencies.

RESPONSIBILITY FOR HEDGING

Plan sponsors must decide who is going to provide the hedging service for them. Currency hedging can be done in-house, using existing expertise. Many organizations will find considerable capabilities for hedging in-house. Then, they must decide whether the experiences and activities in that particular area are appropriate for the type of hedging needed for the investment portfolio. Alternatively, the manager of the underlying securities may be the most appropriate person to do the hedging, because that manager has the complete picture on his or her specific portfolio and can make the currency decision to best complement their style. A third approach is to select a separate, distinct manager for hedging, to be superimposed over the other existing international managers.

All three of these approaches have been used. There are both advantages and disadvantages to each of these approaches. In selecting the appropriate approach to hedging, one must make sure the approach is efficient and that the staff has sufficient expertise to implement it well, taking into consideration the specific fund's characteristics.

HEDGING INSTRUMENTS

There are a variety of instruments that can be used for hedging. The three most commonly used are forward contracts, options, and futures. The use of forward contracts is the least expensive approach and the one that normally is used for passive hedging. Options and futures are also used frequently, particularly when one wants to participate partially in currency movements. They are a little more expensive but are much more useful in the dynamic and active approaches.

One of the key elements a plan sponsor must consider is the cost-benefit trade-off for hedging. The plan sponsor must determine whether that cost to hedging is outweighed by the elimination of the multi-currency risk. The cost is primarily a function of two pieces: trading costs and management costs. Trading costs have been estimated to be between 25 and 100 basis points, depending on the frequency of rebalancing and the types of vehicles used. Management fees are estimated to be between 5 and 20 basis points. Those costs have to be evaluated against the ultimate objective, either to control risk or to improve return.

Establishment of a performance benchmark is critical if the ultimate success or lack of success of a hedging operation is to be determined. A benchmark must be established, the goal specified, and the time horizon considered.

CONCLUSION

The decision on whether to hedge is an issue that any plan sponsor investing outside the United States must consider. It is not an issue that can be answered overnight; it is something that requires detailed analysis and input from a variety of resources. Ultimately, the hedging decision must be based on the needs of the specific fund.

Question and Answer Session

QUESTION: There appears to be a surge of interest in hedging. To what do you attribute this?

PROFFER: I think there is a surge in hedging because people do not want to lose the gains from their investments outside the United States if the dollar begins to strengthen. Consequently, these people are looking at different kinds of approaches to protect that earned return.

RHODES: I agree, but I also think the reasons are broader. The larger plans are thinking about the long-term implications of their policies and how to integrate them into their overall asset allocation procedures. There is probably a strong foundation for the coordination of policies with how to manage the fund most effectively. In today's environment, that process is accelerating because of the strength of the dollar.

QUESTION: Ms. Proffer, how did you determine your estimate of 25 to 100 basis points for the cost of hedging?

PROFFER: I derived this range from several sources. The primary source is actual quotes from managers offering to hedge for various plan sponsors. The low end of the range, 25 basis points, was also quoted in an article published in the *Financial Analysts Journal* [Perold and Schulman 1988]. So rather than give you the various ranges within, I gave you the total breadth of the range. Higher costs frequently are associated with using options and futures in less liquid markets.

RHODES: Our experience indicates that the cost of hedging is more in the 20 basis points area, in terms of rolling hedges and the bid-ask spreads.

QUESTION: Doesn't the hedging of the international exposure offset the effect of diversification, especially if the international sector comprises only 10 to 15 percent of the portfolio?

RHODES: Even if the allocation to foreign assets is only 10 to 15 percent, there will be some loss of diversification between the hedged foreign asset and the domestic asset. But if you are allocating to both foreign equity and foreign fixed-income on a hedged basis, you will benefit substantially from lower correlations among those assets. If you concentrate simply on the equity level and hedge, there is still a drop in the risk level of the total portfolio. Whether to be more or less hedged is a question of risk control and planning. So the plan sponsor, even at a 10 or 15 percent risk level, has to think about what his normal policy is versus what his tactical strategy should be.

QUESTION: How is the dynamic hedging policy implemented?

RHODES: Our manager of option strategies monitors the basket position daily and will execute trades as often as necessary—possibly daily—given the movement of the currencies that are being proxied for our passive portfolios. In fact, intraday transactions have occurred where the currency movement has been substantial in a particular day.

QUESTION: Have you considered short calls?

RHODES: No.

QUESTION: Are hedged international indexes available to use as benchmarks?

PROFFER: Yes, there are hedged indexes. The Salomon Brothers World Government Bond Index is published monthly on a hedged and unhedged basis. The EAFE Index results are also published on both a hedged and unhedged basis. The methodology and the quantitative capability exists to set a normalized benchmark for your portfolio, which is probably more appropriate for larger funds.

QUESTION: What would be an appropriate benchmark? Is it a global or an international benchmark and should it be hedged or otherwise?

PROFFER: The appropriate benchmark depends on the objectives that the fund sets for its hedging strategy. If it is determined that hedging is appropriate for the fund, the benchmark will depend on the purpose of that hedging—to control risk or to produce return. There is not one particular benchmark that is appropriate for everyone. The decision is a function of the long-term targets of the plan, the actual asset allocation, and the objectives of the sponsor.

RHODES: Hedged indexes are beginning to appear.

The Salomon fixed-income indexes are being presented on a fully hedged basis, so a plan sponsor could create a reasonable benchmark proxy for an active manager simply by weighting the dollar-exposed index 50 percent and the fully hedged index 50 percent for a normal target of 50 percent. On the equity side, Morgan Stanley is working on a hedged EAFE index. Some managers, though, are starting to compute their own.

QUESTION: Is there a reason why hedged bond indexes were developed before hedged equity indexes?

RHODES: Yes. Currency risk has a much greater impact on the bond side.

PROFFER: Although it is hard to quote numbers, people often say the currency impact on a bond portfolio is 50 percent and the impact on an international equity portfolio averages around 20 percent, although it has been higher in the recent past. So there is a significant difference in the impact of the currency issue on the ultimate performance characteristics of those two types of asset classes.

QUESTION: Do you see any managers with proven accuracy in predicting currency movements?

RHODES: It is certainly difficult in a short period of time to identify skill statistically in any area of investment, especially in the currency risk area. Nevertheless, some managers have seemed to be able, over substantial periods of time, to add value in the currency risk area. That is the type of manager you would want to implement active currency decisions against a benchmark; you would not want to overlay his strategies or offset his strategies with some other manager making decisions on currency.

QUESTION: Isn't one of the reasons for international equity investing to get foreign currency exposure? And if so, why hedge?

RHODES: If you want to diversify your systematic risk outside the U.S. markets it makes sense to move into non-U.S. markets. Currency risk should be viewed as a separate decision that can be controlled. One can either accept it or reject it, based on normal or tactical strategies. Systems are being developed to allow investors make those decisions separately from the decision to diversify systematic risk into other countries and other markets.

PROFFER: It is true that plan sponsors look at investment outside the United States to participate in the various currencies. The real issue is, will that produce value over time? Research indicates that there is less value and more risk provided by multi-currency exposure. One should also evaluate whether the past 10 years are reflective of what is going to occur in the future. If someone believes that the diversification by currency, as well as the diversification by markets, is what they are really looking for, then hedging is not something they would want to pursue on a continuous basis.

Hedging Decisions Within the Overall Asset Allocation Strategy

Adrian F. Lee

The theme of this presentation is that in the area of international investment, plan sponsors face three asset allocation decisions instead of two. The first is the decision to allocate between domestic assets and international assets, the second is the decision to allocate between international stocks and international bonds, and the third is the decision to allocate between international assets and international currencies. The third decision is a new one for plan sponsors.

In this presentation, I will begin with a review of the traditional asset allocation problem and the approach used by major plan sponsors. Then I will discuss the asset allocation decision from the perspective of allowing the separation of assets and currencies, as provided by currency hedging. Finally, I will present a framework for optimal asset and currency allocation going forward, considering the decision from both the policy level and the tactical level.

I draw three major conclusions from this analysis. First, there are significant benefits to plan sponsors, in terms of risks and rewards, in the simple process of separating the asset allocation decision from the currency allocation decision. Second, the optimal normal, or policy, level of currency exposure may in fact be zero over the long run. This in no way reduces the role of tactical currency management; it simply redefines the neutral position for tactical currency management as a zero level, as opposed to what we had been using before, which is the market capitalization weights of all the currencies they are invested in. The third conclusion is that in this new environment of a fully hedged neutral currency position, the role of tactical currency management becomes the only provider of the actual optimal hedge ratio for currencies. The application of tactical currency management has value added that may, in fact, be directly proportional to currency volatility.

INTERNATIONAL ASSET ALLOCATION

Plan sponsors have tended to approach the decision of the allocation between domestic and international securities in a very compartmentalized way. First, they look at the decision to go international from the point of view of stocks and then from the point of view of bonds. **Figure 1** shows the total returns in U.S. dollars of the major equity markets outside the United States: Japan, the United Kingdom, and West Germany. In terms of returns over the past 10 years, the major markets have outperformed the U.S. dollar market. **Figure 2** shows the standard deviation of returns in U.S. dollars for these markets. The standard deviation of returns calculated in dollars indicates that each individual international equity market has been more risky than the markets in the United States, but that a diversified portfolio of equity markets has been less risky. The world portfolio—that is, U.S. and non-U.S. markets combined—has been the least risky type of equity portfolio available to a U.S. investor. This is the reason many plan sponsors have decided to allocate some portion of their U.S. equity portfolios overseas.

Over the past 10 years, returns in the major international fixed-income markets have outperformed the U.S. fixed-income market. **Figure 3** shows international fixed-income returns. In terms of risk, each individual foreign bond market has been significantly more risky than the U.S. bond market, but, again, a world portfolio of bonds has been the least risky type of bond strategy available. **Figure 4** shows the standard deviation of returns to international fixed-income markets.

Traditionally, plan sponsors have approached the international asset allocation problem by looking at stocks and bonds in isolation. In fact, plan sponsors face a four-way asset allocation decision between U.S. stocks, U.S. bonds, international stocks, and international bonds. **Figure 5** shows the risk-return trade-off for all combinations of U.S. bonds, non-U.S. bonds, U.S. stocks, and non-U.S. stocks. The opportunity set is the area between the lines, not the points along the lines.

Before one can be in a position to address these decisions logically it is important to recognize that, in international investment, returns derive from two separate sources of return: local return and currency return. It is important to allow for the separation these two sources of returns. Unfortunately, these

FIGURE 1. International Equity Markets: Returns in U.S. Dollars (1978-1987)

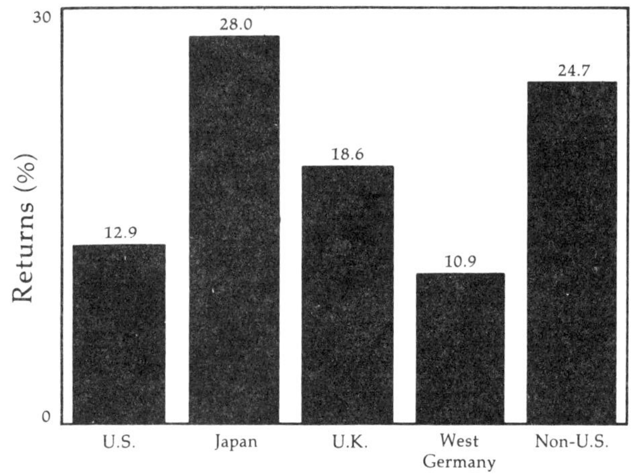

Source: J.P. Morgan Investment Management, Inc.

FIGURE 2. International Equity Markets: Standard Deviation of Returns in U.S. Dollars (1978-1987)

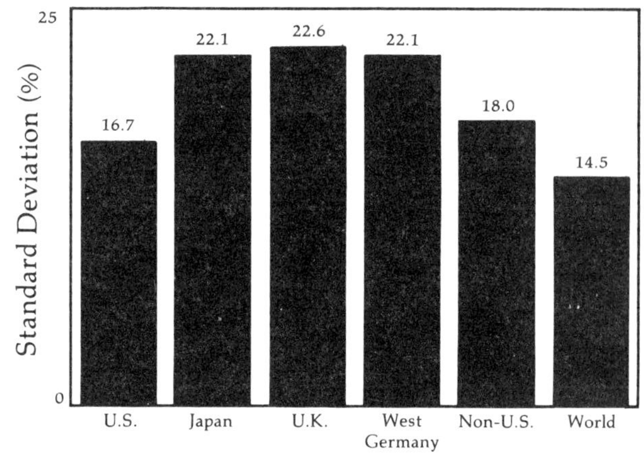

Source: J.P. Morgan Investment Management, Inc.

two decisions are made simultaneously when one purchases a foreign security: If you purchase a foreign security it immediately implies an equal exposure to that foreign currency. **Figure 6** illustrates what those equal exposures have meant for international equities in terms of returns for U.S. investors over the past 10 years. The currency return has been small and rather unsystematic in the sense that it has been positive for one market and negative for another, compared to the local return. **Figure 7** shows the breakdown for fixed-income markets. The results are similar to those of the equity markets. Such results have led many investors to argue that currencies are a small and unsystematic source of long-run return, and that they can be ignored over the long term. This argument, however, ignores the impact of currencies on investment risk.

Total dollar risk may be decomposed into local market risk and currency risk. **Figure 8** illustrates the breakdown of risk across markets. The currency risk is a substantial fraction of the local market risk. For the Japanese equity market, for example, the

FIGURE 3. International Fixed-Income Markets: Returns in U.S. Dollars (1978-1987)

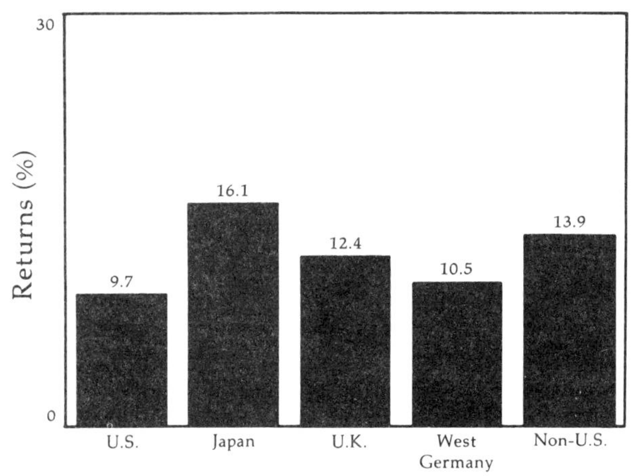

Source: J.P. Morgan Investment Management, Inc.

FIGURE 4. International Fixed-Income Markets: Standard Deviation of Returns in U.S. Dollars (1978-1987)

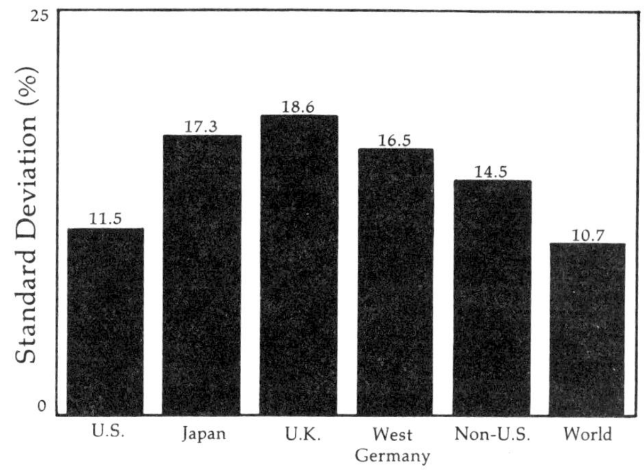

Source: J.P. Morgan Investment Management, Inc.

FIGURE 5. International Equity and Bond Markets: Returns and Risk (1978-1987)

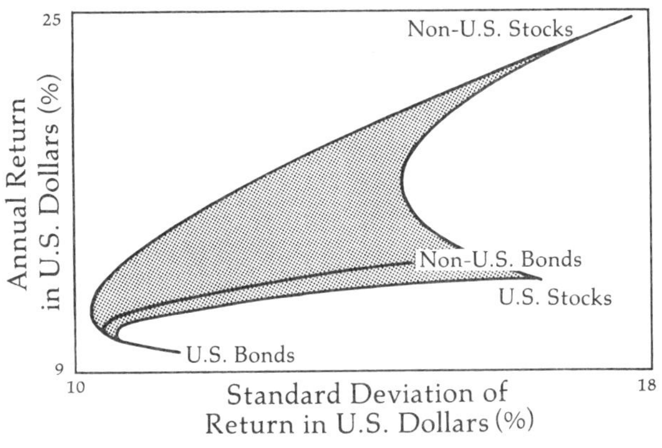

Source: J.P. Morgan Investment Management, Inc.

FIGURE 6. International Equity Markets: Local and Currency Returns (1978-1987)

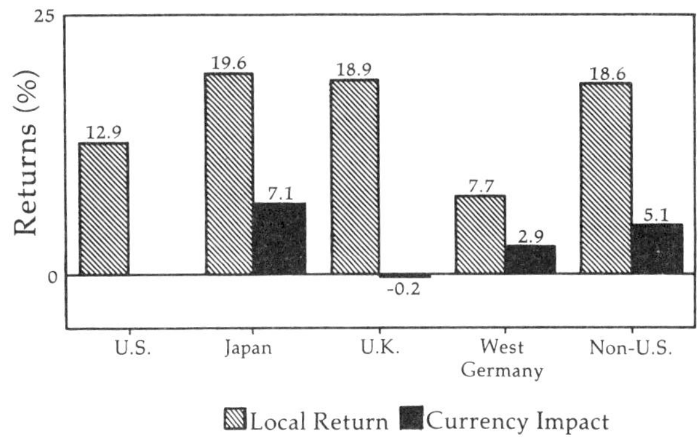

Source: J.P. Morgan Investment Management, Inc.

currency risk is about 80 percent of the local market risk. On a diversified basis over all non-U.S. markets, currency risk does not diversify away and is about 80 or 90 percent of local risk. Figure 8 also illustrates the correlations of equity markets with their own currencies. These correlations are small by most standards, suggesting there is no systematic relationship between local market returns and currency returns.

The international fixed-income markets produce even more dramatic results, as illustrated in **Figure 9.** In these markets, the currency risk is 100 to 200 percent of the local market risk. The correlations for international fixed-income markets are higher than the correlations in the equity market, but they are not high enough for one to argue that the currency and the assets should be taken as two simultaneous and equal decisions. Currencies may be a small, unsystematic source of long-run return; however, they are definitely a systematic and significant source of investment risk. For that reason, currencies in international investing should not be simply assumed: They should be managed, and they should be managed separately from the international asset exposure.

FIGURE 7. International Fixed-Income Markets: Local and Currency Returns (1978-1987)

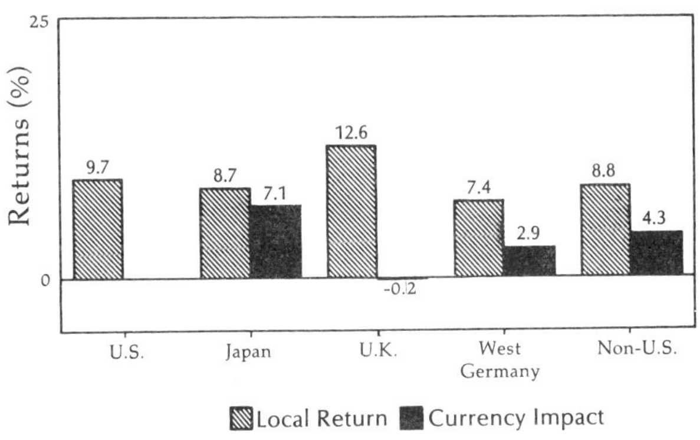

Source: J.P. Morgan Investment Management, Inc.

FIGURE 8. International Equity Markets: Local and Currency Risks (1978-1987)

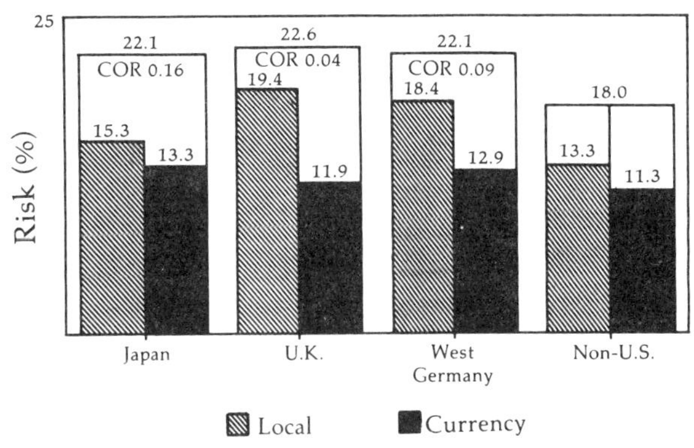

Source: J.P. Morgan Investment Management, Inc.

FIGURE 9. International Fixed-Income Markets: Local and Currency Risks (1978-1987)

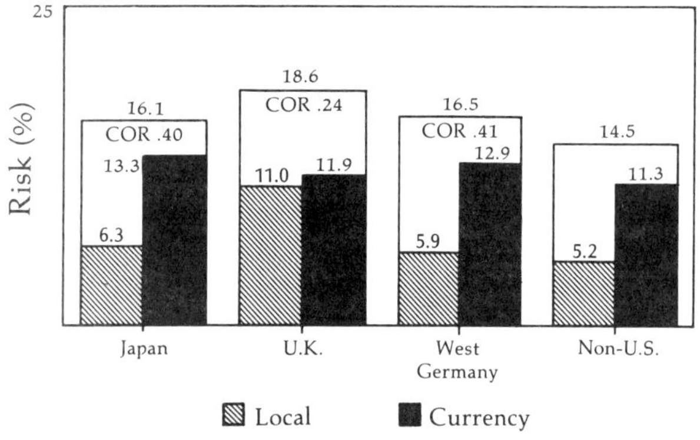

Source: J.P. Morgan Investment Management, Inc.

FIGURE 10. International Equity and Bond Markets: Returns and Risk (1978-1987)

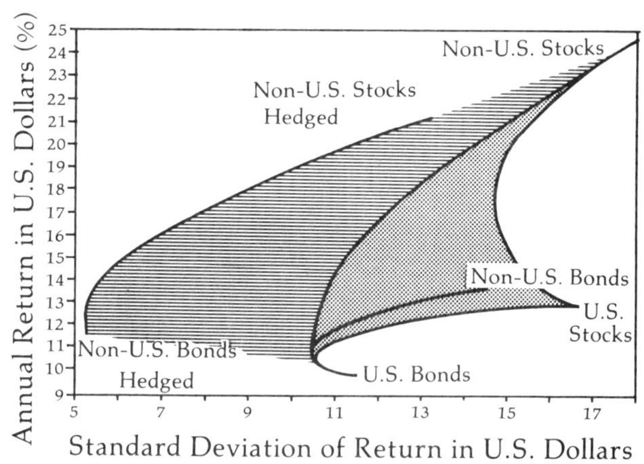

Source: J.P. Morgan Investment Management, Inc.

Currency exposure may be eliminated or reduced by selling the currency forward into the U.S. dollar. The return to a fully hedged asset becomes equal to the local market return plus the forward premium. The forward premium, by definition, is equal to the difference between the U.S. short-term risk-free rate and the foreign short-term risk-free rate for the period of the hedge. This number may be positive or negative.

By continuously rolling over currency hedges, it is possible to create pure foreign assets with currency exposure. **Figure 10** shows the opportunity set available to plan sponsors who are prepared to allow investment in pure international assets. The shift in the opportunity set in Figure 10 compared to Figure 9 is significant. The benefits accrue to plan sponsors who are prepared to separate the long-run asset allocation decision from the long-run currency allocation decision.

The order of magnitude for such a shift is also significant. The shift in risk between non-U.S. stocks and hedged non-U.S. stocks is approximately equal to the shift in risk produced by taking all of one's money out of the U.S. stock market and putting it in the U.S. bond market. The asset allocation implications of hedging are similar to the asset allocation implications of going from U.S. stocks to U.S. bonds. Plan sponsors deliberate for a long time over the U.S. stock/bond decision; they should take just as much time over the hedged/unhedged decision. It is an asset allocation decision.

The same comparison for bonds, hedged or unhedged, indicates that the shift in risk between unhedged international fixed-income and hedged international fixed-income securities is equivalent to taking one's money out of the U.S. bond market and putting it into cash. Again, the hedging decision is significant and should be viewed as an asset allocation decision.

The purpose of investing in international equities and bonds is to diversify. **Table 1** shows the correlation of returns across the different asset categories. Historically, the U.S. equity market and the international equity markets, as defined by EAFE, have shown a 0.39 correlation of monthly return. If that index was hedged by rolling over monthly forward contracts each month, the correlation would rise slightly to 0.54. In other words, hedged assets still offer significant diversification. A similar shift in diversification characteristics can be seen in international fixed-income securities, where the correlation increases slightly, from 0.40 to 0.54. This slight shift in the correlation can be shown mathematically to be swamped by the risk reduction available from hedging; however, the basic point is that inter-

TABLE 1. International Equity and Bond Markets: Correlation of Returns (1978-87)

U.S. stocks	1.00					
U.S. bonds	0.28	1.00				
Non-U.S. stocks	0.39	0.25	1.00			
Non-U.S. bonds	0.02	0.41	0.66	1.00		
Non-U.S. stocks (hedged)	0.54	0.11	0.77	0.08	1.00	
Non-U.S. bonds (hedged)	0.12	0.54	0.39	0.68	0.20	1.00

Source: J.P. Morgan Investment Management, Inc.

national diversification does not result simply from currency exposure, but from exposure to foreign markets that react to foreign influences.

An interesting diversification benefit accrues to hedging. The correlation between international stocks and international bonds, unhedged, is relatively high, because when you buy a foreign security—either a bond or a stock—you are also buying the foreign currency. There is a high correlation (0.66) between unhedged international fixed-income securities and unhedged international equities. This, in part, has been why plan sponsors have hesitated to put large sums of money into international fixed-income markets, unhedged, particularly when they already have international equities in their portfolio. If both of those assets are hedged, the correlation drops from 0.66 to 0.20, which is similar to the bond-stock correlation that one expects. Hedging, then, for those who have international assets of both stocks and bonds, has a significant diversification benefit.

A FRAMEWORK FOR OPTIMAL ASSET AND CURRENCY ALLOCATION

Having allowed conceptually for the separation of the asset and currency decisions, there are several steps in the process of determining an optimal asset and currency allocation. The first step is to separate the asset and currency allocation decisions, conceptually. The next step is to identify the asset classes and, for each of those asset classes, develop expected returns, risks, and covariances.

The following example illustrates the process. In this example, we have defined U.S. stocks and U.S. bonds as separate asset classes, with expected returns and risk as given in **Table 2**. Non-U.S. stocks and non-U.S. bonds are defined as separate asset classes. All have similar risks and returns and risk-return relationships. We also allow two new asset classes: hedged foreign stocks and hedged foreign bonds. The risks of the hedged asset classes are about 25 percent less for equities and about 60 percent less for bonds—which is approximately the historical volatility reduction realized through hedging.

On the return side, we assume that hedged and unhedged returns will be the same in the long run. These assumptions are based on four factors. First, because it is not logical to expect the forward exchange markets to be continuously surprised, in either direction, hedged returns should equal unhedged returns. Second, if one believes that purchasing power parity is a rational expectation, and that real interest rates should be approximately equal across markets in the long run, then hedged returns will be equal to unhedged returns. Third, there is little evidence in the academic literature that currency risk is a capital asset risk that should be rewarded. According to theory, equity risk should be rewarded through its beta and expected return, and credit risk should be rewarded through higher yields. There is no theory on how currency risk should be priced. Finally, the argument that currencies are a zero-sum game—for example, the return the Japanese investor makes through currency gains must be the loss that the U.S. investor makes through currency returns—implies that there cannot be simultaneously positive long-run returns on both sides of the contract. Based on this type of evidence, there is no logical reason to assume *a priori* that hedged should outperform or underperform unhedged international investments. This assumption is relaxed later to show what implications would follow if this assumption was allowed.

TABLE 2. Optimal Asset and Currency Allocation Long-run Equilibrium Assumptions

	Compound Return	*Annual Standard Deviation*
U.S. stocks	10.5%	18.0%
U.S. bonds	7.5	9.0
Non-U.S. stocks	11.0	20.0
Non-U.S. bonds	7.5	11.0
Non-U.S. stocks (hedged)	11.0	15.0
Non-U.S. bonds (hedged)	7.5	4.5

Source: J.P. Morgan Investment Management, Inc.

Taking these inputs, we can use optimization techniques to develop an analysis of the marginal value added of each separate asset class. **Figure 11** shows the optimal normal portfolios. The expected return-risk opportunity set available to a plan sponsor who considers only U.S. stocks and U.S. bonds is on the far right. The return to U.S. bonds is about 7.5 percent and risk about 9 or 10 percent, as shown on the bottom left corner of the figure. The return to U.S. stocks is in the top right corner.

The opportunity set shifts to the left when international equities are included. That is basically the case for international equity diversification. The effect of an allocation to international fixed-income, unhedged, is minimal, and only at lower levels of risk. As I noted earlier, because of the very high correlation between fixed-income and international equities, it does not make sense to put a lot of international fixed-income into a portfolio that already has international equities.

The opportunity set shifts significantly, particularly at moderate or lower levels of risk, when an allocation of fully hedged international fixed-income

FIGURE 11. Optimal Normal Portfolios: No Constraints

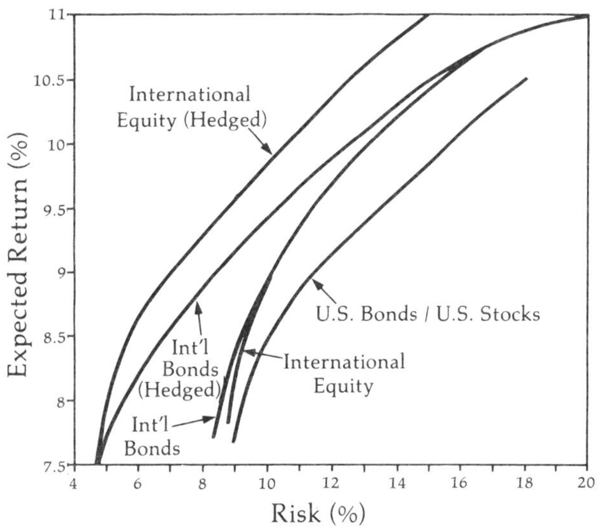

Source: J.P. Morgan Investment Management, Inc.

FIGURE 12. Optimal Normal Portfolios

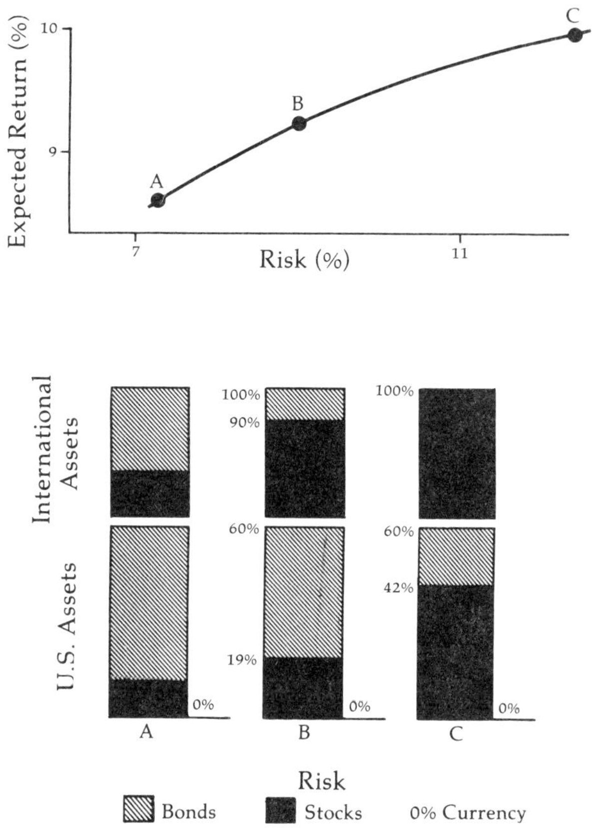

Source: J.P. Morgan Investment Management, Inc.

securities is included. Finally, the inclusion of fully hedged international equities results in another shift in the risk-reward opportunity set.

This analysis shows two things. First, the case for international fixed-income is difficult to make unless it is hedged. Second, the impact of hedging is approximately equal to the original case for international equity diversification. Hedging is as major an issue as diversification itself.

When constraints are added, the results of the optimization are not significantly different. We looked at whether hedging is optimal at all levels of risk, assuming different asset allocations. The portfolio is constrained to a minimum 60 percent allocation to U.S. assets. In **Figure 12**, portfolio A represents the optimal portfolio with a 60 percent allocation to domestic assets, 40 percent to international, and zero to currencies. At that level of risk, it is optimal to hedge all exposure to currencies. All of the international equities and all of the international bonds are fully hedged. At higher levels of risk, the asset allocation changes within our domestic and international portfolio, away from bonds and toward stocks, but the currency exposure remains at zero. This suggests that it is optimal to fully hedge all foreign currency exposures at all levels of risk.

It may be instructive to focus for a moment on the exact formula for optimal hedging strategies. **Table 3** shows the analytical formula for the optimal hedge ratio. The last two terms have tended to be positive. Then, if one assumes that the expected currency return is equal to the forward premium, which is not an irrational starting point, the optimal hedge ratio is greater than one. In other words, one should hedge more than 100 percent of currency exposure.

It would be nice to know how much currency return has to exceed the forward premium to make some currency exposure in an international portfolio desirable. Let us examine an international portfolio—one invested 100 percent in international assets—and define a number called the "currency surprise." The currency surprise is the expected currency return minus the forward premium. If this number is positive, the currency return is expected to be higher than the forward premium; if it is negative, the currency is expected to depreciate by more than the forward premium. We saw that when we expected this number to be zero, it was optimal to have no currency exposure in the portfolio, or, in other words, to fully hedge it. **Figure 13** shows the optimal asset and currency allocation under alternative currency surprises. If this currency surprise number is 2 percent, then the optimal allocation of the portfolio to currency exposure is 32 percent, taking into account all covariance factors. If

TABLE 3. Optimal Hedging Strategies

Assume one asset and two countries.

Total portfolio return (T) = ωD + (1 - ω)[L + C(1 - h) + hFP]

where:
D = domestic asset return
L = foreign local asset return
C = foreign currency appreciation
FP = forward currency premium
ω = proportion invested domestically
h = proportion of foreign currency exposure hedged

It can be shown that h* (optimal hedge ratio) =

$$1 - \frac{(E(C) - FP)}{2\lambda(1-\omega)Var(C)} + \frac{\omega}{(1-\omega)}\frac{Cov(D.C.)}{Var(C)} + \frac{1}{(1-\omega)}\frac{Cov(L.C.)}{Var(C)}$$

Source: J.P. Morgan Investment Management, Inc.

currencies are expected to exceed the forward premium and the return by 4 to 6 percent, then up to 45 percent of the portfolio may be allocated to currency exposure.

Two conclusions emerge from this analysis. First, one must have a very optimistic view of the long-run returns from currencies in excess of the forward premium to justify a fully unhedged or fully currency-exposed portfolio. Unhedging imputes an expected return by the plan sponsor to currency return, over the long run, that may be excessive. Second, because we know in practice that, over the short run, currency returns differ significantly—by 5 to 20 percent—from the forward premium, we know that the optimal hedge ratio over time will vary significantly. It can be zero, 50 percent, or 100 percent. The role of tactical currency management is to determine this amount. Because of the sensitivity of the optimal hedge ratio to this currency return number, the tactical currency manager's role becomes critical in providing to the plan sponsor the actual optimal hedges through time.

Our research into optimal tactical hedging has shown that, under certain assumptions, the value added by a manager who uses optimal tactical hedging techniques is proportional to currency volatility. To the extent that currency variance is expected to continue, the value added to tactical currency management will be significant.

CONCLUSION

International investors face three major asset allocation decisions: domestic assets versus international assets, international equities versus international bonds, and international assets versus international currencies. Our research suggests that there are significant benefits associated with the process of separating the long-run asset allocation decision from the long-run currency allocation decision. The correct long-run or normal currency allocation exposure may be fully hedged. In this environment of fully hedged normal portfolios, the role of tactical currency management is to provide the actual optimal hedge ratio, which at any point in time is unlikely to be 100 percent hedged. Finally, the value added in this process is related directly to the currency volatility.

There are several qualifications to what I have said. First, this analysis has not included transaction costs. Our research suggests that in hedging there are four sources of transaction costs: costs in the spot market for hedging, costs of rollover in the forward market, market impact costs, and cash flow-related costs. The sum total of those transaction costs, in our opinion, should not exceed 25 basis points.

Second, it has been argued that the inflation hedge characteristics of currencies are desirable. Undertaking this analysis in real returns did not yield very different results. It appears that, although it is logical to assume currencies are a U.S. inflation hedge, there is not enough empirical evidence to justify that this relationship is sufficient to warrant assuming currency risk.

Finally, I have defined risk in terms of total portfolio risk. This does not necessarily have direct application to plan sponsors who define risk in terms of asset and liability mismatching.

FIGURE 13. Optimal Asset and Currency Allocation Under Alternative Currency Surprises

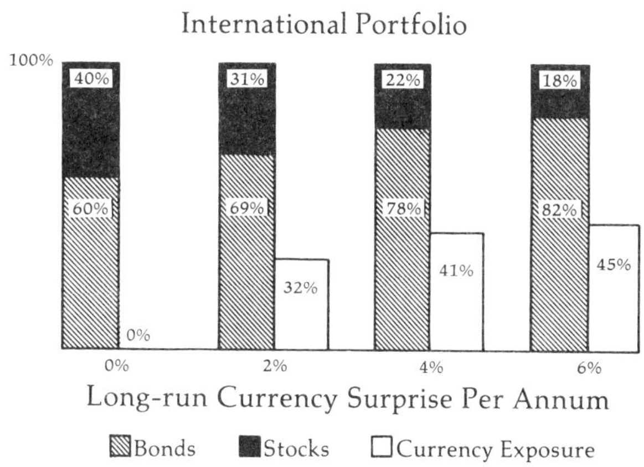

Source: J.P. Morgan Investment Management, Inc.

Question and Answer Session

QUESTION: Are your measurement data monthly, quarterly, or daily? Would the results change if you used a different time period?

LEE: The data are all monthly. We simulated all our returns monthly, and our hedge contracts were monthly forward contracts rolled over.

QUESTION: Does the optimal allocation for currency hedging change as you go from nominal to real inflation-adjusted returns?

LEE: I don't think there is much change. There is some evidence, but not enough, that currencies are an inflation hedge. Most of the causes of global inflation are not local; they affect all currencies simultaneously. To the extent that inflation is a global phenomenon, currencies are not a hedge against inflation.

QUESTION: Most international analysis rests heavily on the assumption of normal distributions of returns. Is this realistic?

LEE: The assumptions of normality and lognormality relate to whether an investor considers utility in terms of risks and returns, as opposed to risks, returns, skewness, and kurtosis. We have made no explicit assumption about the distribution of returns. There is evidence that security returns internationally are just as lognormally distributed as they are domestically. There is not a lot of evidence to suggest that currency returns are normal, however. The analysis will not be affected as long as investors make their decisions on the basis of risk and return. If they don't, things get exceedingly complicated, and we have to measure things like skewness and kurtosis.

QUESTION: What does the hedge ratio of more than one actually mean?

LEE: There are good reasons for assuming a positive relationship between currencies and markets. Currencies are stronger when countries can afford to lower their interest rates, and that is good for the equity markets. So when you buy in the equity market, you also buy an embedded bet on the currency. It is not systematic, but there is a relationship. If you really want to get rid of all currency exposure, you have to over-hedge the international equity exposure. It is probably economically very sensible to hedge more than 100 percent, but it is probably not allowed by most plan sponsors to hedge more than their asset exposure. That may change, and maybe people will hedge more than 100 percent of their foreign currency exposure, going forward.

QUESTION: If forward foreign exchange rates are based on intracountry interest rate differentials, how can the international fixed-income decision be separated from the hedging decision?

LEE: The forward rate is defined by the market at any point in time. It is like a fixed premium or discount that you pay for hedging. It is not a transaction cost, but it is like a transaction cost; it is a fixed number. To the extent you believe that interest rate differentials explain currency returns and local market returns, there is a link.

QUESTION: Is it appropriate to look at risk on a month-to-month basis when, in fact, many of us are supposed to be representing funds that have long-term time horizons?

LEE: This is a difficult issue. An investor's risk preference or risk tolerance is important in the actual empirical solution of problems of asset allocation. An investor who can take a lot of risk in the long run will have 100 percent equities in his portfolio; one who can not will have 50 percent equities and 50 percent bonds. So our actual numerical analysis is contingent on a risk preference. Whether you use monthly returns or annual returns does not affect the outcome. We have annualized our returns to come up with risk parameters over the one-year or one-quarter horizon. As long as the data are independent, that is a fair way to measure the relationships. Also, it is better to have fewer observations, because that gives you a better handle on some of the covariances and risks. Underlying this is the notion that hedging does not matter to risk-insensitive investors. Such plan sponsors have to justify why they are exposing themselves to a risk that does not appear to be rewarded, no matter how small. Unless risk is not a negative factor for an investor, and there are very few who can say that, then he has to justify the imputed excess return he is putting into currencies. Because the transaction costs are so small, it is very difficult to justify a fully unhedged position, no matter what your risk preferences are. Certainly the numbers change, depending on risk preferences, but the relationship of an unrewarded risk is there. If we started this analysis in 1974 without historical data, we would really have to seek out a logical theory of why currency risk is rewarded just like equity risk or credit risk should be rewarded.

QUESTION: Many companies are very exposed to foreign markets and foreign currencies in their basic businesses. How do we measure the currency distribution of our portfolio in practice?

LEE: There are two aspects to this problem. It is important to define the total analysis in terms of the currency the liabilities are in. Most defined benefit pension plans have their liabilities defined in U.S. dollars. To the extent that liabilities are actually multi-currency, there is no risk in going into foreign currencies. One could argue that a defined contribution plan actually has a multi-currency liability. A defined contribution plan is designed to provide income for people after retirement in an asset-accumulation way, and what they spend their money on is, in fact, their need for foreign currencies. If they are going to buy French clothes and West German cars in retirement, they will need French francs and West German marks in their portfolio. So, to the extent that the liabilities are multi-currency, this whole analysis does not apply, and I have not really addressed that question. Second, if companies are really multinational, they have actual global currencies in their equity price. That is a very interesting area of research—when you buy IBM, to what extent are you actually buying all the currencies and all the equity markets in the world? I do not have an answer for that one.

Measuring the Effectiveness of Currency Hedging Strategies

Richard C. Carr, CFA

Measuring the effectiveness of currency hedging strategies is a new and extremely complex topic. Changing from an unhedged portfolio to a fully hedged portfolio alters the characteristics of that portfolio and, therefore, affects the asset allocation decision. In this presentation, I will discuss several aspects of the policy considerations of hedging, including the advantages, the costs, the impact on the surplus of a retirement plan, and the benchmarks that one might use in managing portfolios. I will also discuss some asset allocation ideas.

There is probably no one answer to the question of whether to hedge. Clearly, different factors should be considered in making the decision. The effectiveness of currency hedging is a function of its impact on performance, but performance is obviously a function of the investor's objectives. I will discuss the effectiveness of hedged portfolios versus unhedged portfolios in a policy sense, rather than in a strategic or tactical sense.

HEDGED VERSUS UNHEDGED PORTFOLIOS

The major argument in favor of hedging is that it lowers volatility. The hedged portfolio is less volatile than the unhedged portfolio because it eliminates currency fluctuations. Returns should be unchanged when one moves from the unhedged portfolio to the hedged portfolio, because in a real sense, or an inflation-adjusted sense, currency does not make any difference. Purchasing power parity tells us that hedging should not change returns in the long run. The statement on risk is fairly obvious and well-documented. One of the problems with the documentation, however, is that most of the studies are based on fairly recent data. Some researchers have attempted to extrapolate the past into the future, but we think it is dangerous to base policy norms simply on the statistical evidence from the past 10 to 15 years. After all, floating exchange rates are relatively new, and few investors would want to make any serious decisions based on data from such a short time period. The decision should ultimately be based on forecasts that will be stable over time.

The effectiveness of hedged versus unhedged portfolios is influenced by other considerations as well, including the higher correlations with U.S. assets, the added costs, and the slight loss of diversification.

There is a loss of diversification with hedging continuously because, in effect, you are creating a synthetic U.S. instrument. Because of the arbitrage in the forward exchange markets, the yields ought to be the same as for the U.S. assets. Thus, all that is gained in a hedged portfolio versus a U.S. portfolio is the variation in local market returns from the U.S. returns. This loss of diversification is more than offset by the elimination of currency volatility, but it is a factor to consider.

The correlations of local markets with the U.S. market are low, and there seems to be no tendency for those correlations to rise. On the other hand, some of the arguments for using hedged portfolios are based on assumptions about the local market risk or volatility—for example, that low local market risk will continue in the future. That may not be a safe assumption, however. For example, will the Japanese bond market continue to be less volatile than the U.S. bond market?

There are some added costs associated with hedged portfolios. We approach these costs from the standpoint of managing large sums of money on a fully hedged basis with regular rollovers. There are no commissions in the foreign exchange markets, but there are transaction costs because of spreads, and market impact costs that rise with volume. The market impact costs are similar to those incurred when one trades large amounts of equities or bonds. There are also cash-flow considerations. Hedging can require an inflow of cash at settlement, or money can come out when successful forward exchange contracts are completed. This creates additional transaction costs, because securities must be purchased or sold to balance the cash flow. In our estimation, all those costs can total 40 to 50 basis points per year, assuming that every month you roll over the hedge in a neutral, passive way. This is not a huge cost, but it should be factored into asset allocation policies. For example, assume that over the long term, U.S. bonds, non-U.S. bonds, and fully hedged non-U.S. bonds will each return 8.5 percent. To account for the added costs of hedging, 40 to 50 basis points should be subtracted from the hedged return, for a total return of closer to 8 percent. This changes the recommended asset allocations, because optimization models tend to be very sensitive to small changes in assumptions.

PORTFOLIO RISK

Risk should be evaluated for the total portfolio, not just the international portion. **Figure 1** shows the forecast risk of global bond portfolios, hedged versus unhedged, and illustrates the change in risk as the proportion invested in the U.S. bond market is decreased. The risk reduction from using non-U.S. bonds is not huge; it occurs only with relatively small amounts of non-U.S. bonds. When more non-U.S. unhedged bonds are added, risk actually goes up. We assume here that the returns on the bonds will be the same, whether they are hedged or unhedged, U.S. or non-U.S.

Clearly, hedging is better, as evidenced by the fact that risk is lower for the hedged portfolio line. But there is not a big difference when international bonds represent only a small percentage of the portfolio. In fact, investing 10 percent in non-dollar bonds reduces risk by only 8 basis points. This is advantageous, but it is not dramatic. These results are based on our assumptions about the future—on forecast risk—rather than on past data.

Figure 2 shows the forecast risk of global equity portfolios. There is a substantial risk reduction from introducing international equities in both the hedged and unhedged cases. Hedging lowers risk, as one would expect. The difference, however, is not very great until 30 or 40 percent of the portfolio is in international equities. In fact, given our assumptions, at the 10 percent of portfolio level, risk is reduced by only one basis point.

Volatility is the key factor—the question is, which volatility is important? No one likes volatility; we would all rather reduce it as long as there is no reduction in return. **Figure 3** illustrates asset volatility over the period 1974 through 1988. The figure shows the risk-return frontier for a portfolio of U.S. and hedged international assets compared to U.S. and unhedged international assets. The hedged line is superior. Historical data indicate that hedging makes sense because it reduces risk.

Some plan sponsors, though not all, also want to consider the difference between the assets and liabilities of a retirement plan, or surplus. **Figure 4** shows an efficient frontier when the assets of a hypothetical retirement plan are combined with its active liability (the liability for members of the retirement plan who are still employed). We used a variation of the methodology outlined in an article by Bostock, Wooley, and Duffy (1989) to simulate changes in the liabilities over time. Assuming a static company, work force, and age distribution, we grew the active liabilities at the inflation rate and then discounted the liability stream back to the present using historical yield curves. Repeating this procedure quarterly over the same time period as was used in Figure 3 shows how the liabilities would have changed as the asset markets changed. This then allows us to calculate correlations between assets and liabilities and to examine the risk-return aspects in an efficient frontier sense.

The results for assets less active liability are dramatically different than for assets only. In fact, the hedged international portfolio is not superior to the unhedged international portfolio. Many plan sponsors do not want to consider only the assets; they

FIGURE 1. Forecast Risk of Global Bond Portfolios: Hedged Versus Unhedged

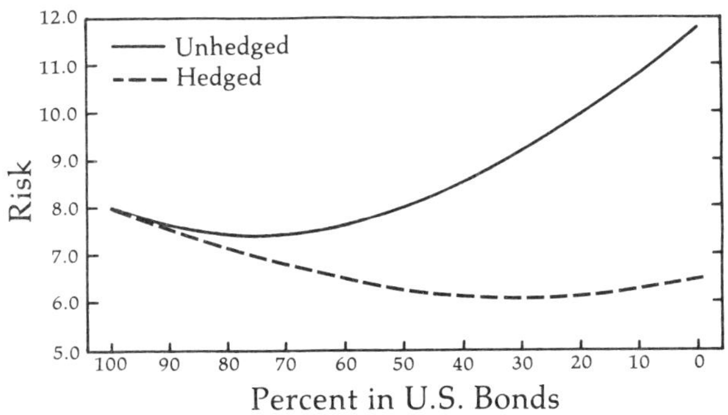

Source: First Chicago Investment Advisors

FIGURE 2. Forecast Risk of Global Equity Portfolios: Hedged Versus Unhedged

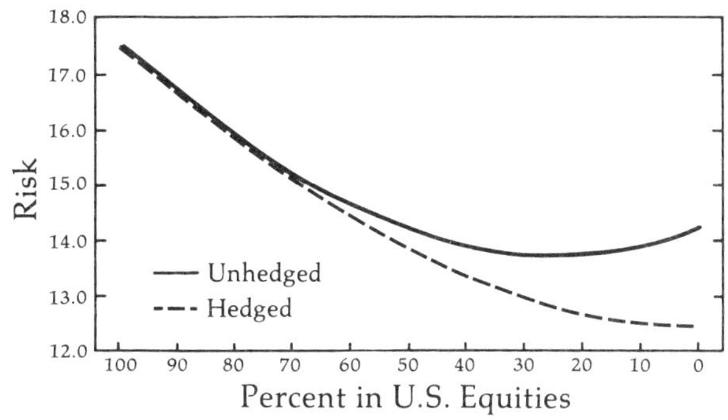

Source: First Chicago Investment Advisors

FIGURE 3. Historical Efficient Frontiers: Assets Only

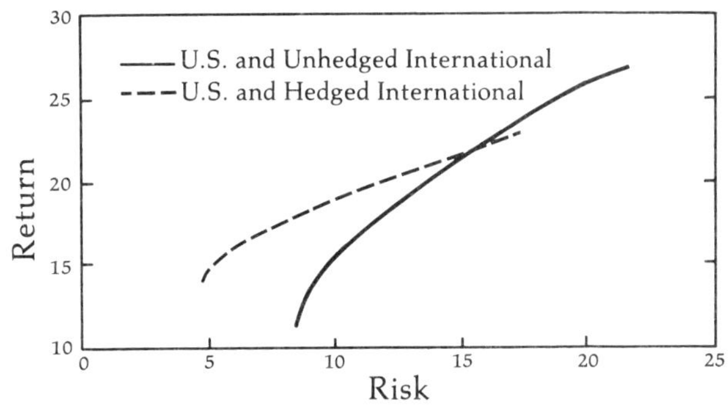

Source: First Chicago Investment Advisors

FIGURE 4. Historical Efficient Frontiers: Assets Less Active Liability

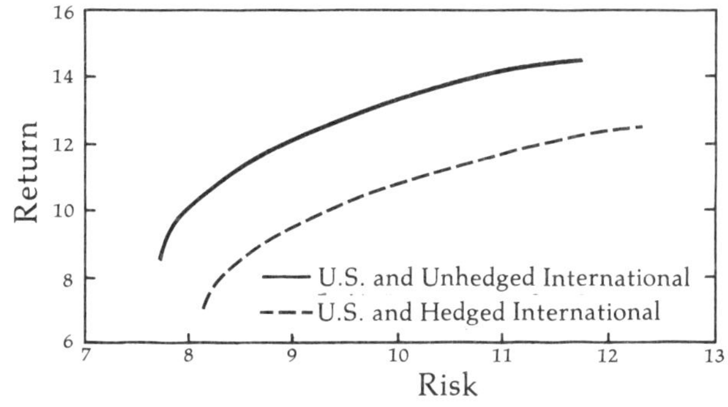

Source: First Chicago Investment Advisors

want to think about the liabilities as well and the effects of international diversification on the surplus. In this framework, high correlations between assets and liabilities are desirable, because the assets are viewed as a hedge. This is somewhat contrary to the usual asset allocation notion of seeking low correlations.

This technique can also be used to analyze the efficient frontier for assets less the retired liability. Obviously the retired liabilities are fixed—a company knows what it has to pay someone when they are retired—so these liabilities behave more like bonds. **Figure 5** shows the efficient frontier for the surplus over retired liability. There is a difference between the hedged and the unhedged frontiers, but it is not significant.

THE ASSET ALLOCATION DECISION

The asset allocation policy decision is also affected by whether one hedges. Three elements should be considered in an asset allocation model: the correlation among the assets, the expected return, and the standard deviation, or volatility, of returns from each asset. Currency is a more significant factor with bonds than with equities, so I will begin with bonds. **Table 1** shows our forecast correlations between the various bond markets of the world, on both an unhedged and hedged basis. As an example, the correlation between West Germany and the United States, on an unhedged basis, is 0.35. On a hedged basis, in our estimation, it will rise to 0.75. Again, one might argue over the exact numbers, but no one would disagree that the correlations are higher once hedging is introduced on a continuous basis.

The next element to be considered in asset allocation is standard deviation. **Table 2** shows forecast standard deviation in a normal, or equilibrium, sense over a long period for hedged and unhedged bonds, country by country. The United States is the point of reference. The standard deviation for unhedged bonds should be high—it has been higher than U.S. bonds in the past because of the currency element. If the currency element is eliminated by hedging, the standard deviation will be lower in each country. Versus the United States, it will be relatively higher in countries like the United Kingdom, which has a more volatile interest rate pattern, and lower in other countries, for example West Germany and Japan.

Other forecasts depend on assumptions. For example, will the standard deviations of those local markets remain the same in the future? Will they stay as low as they have been in the past? We are assuming there is some continuity—for example,

FIGURE 5. Historical Efficient Frontiers: Assets Less Retired Liability

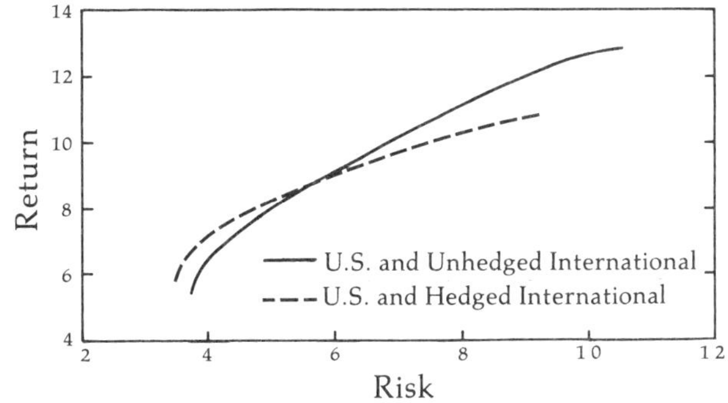

Source: First Chicago Investment Advisors

TABLE 1. Unhedged Versus (Hedged) Bonds: Forecast Correlations

	Canada	*West Germany*	*Japan*	*United Kingdom*	*United States*
Canada	1.00 (1.00)				
West Germany	0.25 (0.70)	1.00 (1.00)			
Japan	0.35 (0.50)	0.75 (0.65)	1.00 (1.00)		
United Kingdom	0.35 (0.45)	0.50 (0.55)	0.55 (0.50)	1.00 (1.00)	
United States	0.85 (0.95)	0.35 (0.75)	0.35 (0.50)	0.30 (0.45)	1.00 (1.00)

Source: First Chicago Investment Advisors

lower volatility in Japan and West Germany and higher volatility in the United Kingdom

The forecast risk premium, however, should not change. Therefore, returns should not change in the long run between the hedged and unhedged portfolios. The risk premium is essentially set by the local investor, so it should be the same on an unhedged and a hedged basis, but it will vary from country to country. **Table 3** shows our forecast risk premia by country.

Based on these factors, one can determine normal portfolios. **Table 4** shows a normal optimal portfolio for non-U.S. bonds, assuming there are no hedging transaction costs. This table demonstrates that the composition of the normal portfolio will change when you move to a fully hedged policy. A similar exercise was performed for equities. **Table 5** shows the normal portfolio for non-U.S. equities. Based on some typical assumptions for international equities and using an optimal analysis, we can demonstrate that the country composition of a normal portfolio of hedged equities is different than the composition of unhedged equities.

This raises a number of questions regarding the concept of using a currency overlay manager. There will be a conflict when the currency overlay manager has as his norm the fully hedged benchmark and the underlying manager of the securities has as his norm the unhedged benchmark. Further, one must consider the practical problems of two managers operating independently on different assumptions. For example, consider the conflict when the active currency overlay manager assumes that the U.S. dollar is going to continue to decline, and the underlying security manager chooses countries and stocks assuming that the U.S. dollar is going to stabilize or go up.

The asset allocation decision is impacted in several ways by hedging. First, as we saw, the composition of the normal portfolio changes. Second, asset allocation policies will be different for hedged and unhedged assets. One would be more willing to take on more international assets when they are hedged (and therefore less risky).

These results make one question why market capitalization weights are being used. When one manages money against benchmarks outside the United States, one uses market-capitalization-weighted benchmarks, probably because we are accustomed to using them in the United States. In the United States, there are market-capitalization-weighted benchmarks for both U.S. stocks and U.S. bonds. But when we make asset allocation policies in the United States, we do not work on the basis of market capitalization. If we did, we would probably have more bonds than stocks in a normal portfolio, because the U.S. bond market is larger than the U.S. equity market. Instead, most investors use the typical 60/40 mix of U.S. equities to U.S. bonds because equities provide a higher return. In asset allocation models, we use investment characteristics rather than size. But when we construct benchmarks outside the United States and compare one country to another, we use the same market capitalization weights.

Market capitalization weights make sense in an efficient market; however, markets may be efficient within each country, but may not be efficient across

TABLE 2. Forecast Standard Deviation

	Unhedged Bonds	*Hedged Bonds*
Canada	14.0	11.5
West Germany	15.0	5.5
Japan	16.0	5.5
United Kingdom	18.0	11.5
United States	8.0	8.0

Source: First Chicago Investment Advisors

TABLE 3. Forecast Risk Premium

	Unhedged Bonds	*Hedged Bonds*
Canada	2.6	2.6
West Germany	1.5	1.5
Japan	1.2	1.2
United Kingdom	2.6	2.6
United States	1.9	1.9

Source: First Chicago Investment Advisors

TABLE 4. Normal Portfolio: Non-U.S. Bonds

	Unhedged Bonds (%)	*Hedged Bonds (%)*
Canada	50	15
West Germany	20	45
Japan	5	15
United Kingdom	25	25
	100	100

Source: First Chicago Investment Advisors

TABLE 5. Normal Portfolio: Non-U.S. Equities

	Unhedged Equities (%)	*Hedged Equities (%)*
Canada	30	15
West Germany	35	40
Japan	15	30
United Kingdom	20	15
	100	100

Source: First Chicago Investment Advisors

markets. Perhaps the best way to think about allocations outside the United States is not on the basis of market capitalization weights but on the basis of the long-term investment characteristics of each market, which is the way one would approach the allocation decision between U.S. equities, U.S. bonds, and other assets.

To optimize a non-U.S. portfolio, one would have to consider the United States as well. In Table 4, Canada ends up being a relatively attractive unhedged market because the returns are similar to those of the United States, the correlation with the other markets is low, and Canada has less volatility because the Canadian dollar is more closely tied to the U.S. dollar than a number of other currencies. So Canada looks attractive because we are examining only non-U.S. markets. But when the United States is added in a global context, the attraction of Canada drops.

Investors rarely think about non-U.S. markets by themselves; they usually think about the non-U.S. markets versus the U.S. market. Assume that the best policy for a global equity portfolio is to have 75 percent in the United States and then find the optimal combination of markets for the remaining 25 percent. That combination will differ from one where 90 percent of the equities is in the United States and 10 percent is in the non-U.S. markets.

A final issue is whether to consider all the countries combined into one. Why do U.S. investors think in terms of a single asset class outside the United States? Everyone knows that the behavior and characteristics of the markets are different. In the future, plan sponsors and managers will begin to move away from thinking about the non-U.S. markets as one entity and will begin to do asset allocation on a disaggregated basis. They will consider the United States versus Japan versus the United Kingdom versus continental Europe. This approach makes more sense, although it raises a number of questions in terms of practical implementation.

CONCLUSION

Hedging offers advantages for those who are sensitive to interim currency volatility and for those who have a very large exposure to international assets, especially non-dollar fixed-income assets. Hedging also makes sense for those who are not concerned with the surplus of a retirement fund and for those who are prepared to use a different set of country weights for the benchmark. Finally, hedging makes sense for those who are prepared to consider a different set of asset allocation weights for their policy.

On the other hand, if an investor is not concerned with interim currency volatility, thinks currency is a wash and perhaps not so important, is only investing 5 to 10 percent internationally, or is not investing much in non-dollar fixed-income assets, hedging still offers an advantage, but not much of one. In addition, if an investor is concerned with the management of the surplus of a retirement fund, he or she probably will not be inclined to establish a fully hedged benchmark policy. Or if the investor does not want to think differently about benchmarks and country weights, hedging should not be adopted.

In conclusion, there is no one doctrinaire answer to the question of whether or not to hedge. The effectiveness of hedging is a function of many considerations, several of which are outlined in this presentation.

Question and Answer Session

QUESTION: Please provide some clarification on the way you classify the liabilities and the methodology used to match the liabilities against the hedged and unhedged portfolios.

CARR: This is a complex issue. To get a stream of liabilities, we used a model of a company that was static—that is, it did not add or reduce the number of employees. We assumed the liabilities would grow over time by an inflation rate. That stream of liabilities was discounted back to the present to determine a present value of those future liabilities. The discount rate was based on the yield curves at the time. This was done on a quarterly basis. Pension asset values are also available on a quarterly basis. Next, we calculated the difference between the assets and the liabilities and computed the returns. Standard deviations and correlations were calculated from the series of returns. From that information, an efficient frontier was determined. I suggest that interested people read the article by Bostock, Wooley, and Duffy [1989].

QUESTION: You said that Canada has a particularly high weighting for unhedged bonds because returns are highly correlated with U.S. bonds. Isn't this precisely why one would want a light weighting of Canadian bonds for a U.S. portfolio?

CARR: Yes, that is correct. My exercise was simply to look at the non-U.S. market in a vacuum, without any U.S. assets. If the U.S. assets are included, the attractiveness of Canada declines.

QUESTION: Is it not true that the argument for a non-capitalization-weighted benchmark is unrelated to hedging? If markets are not globally efficient, capitalization weights may not be suitable, whether or not foreign exchange risk is hedged.

CARR: That is an interesting question. It seems to me that the characteristics of a portfolio change when it is hedged, but that statement is premised on certain assumptions about efficiency.

QUESTION: What methodology is used to forecast risk premiums, correlations, and standard deviations?

CARR: We used history to forecast the future. We generally assumed the correlations would not change in the future. On a rolling correlation basis, there is evidence that correlations are still low and not changing. It is conceivable that one might make some changes in the future, for example within the European markets after 1992. We also assumed that there probably would not be many differences in the standard deviations in the future, but, again, sometimes markets can change. For example, the Japanese bond market in the 1980s is a lot different from the Japanese bond market in the 1970s, when the government had a tighter control over interest rates and the financial markets were less integrated into the world. To determine the risk premium, we tried to ascertain whether each market was integrated or segmented. We made the general assumption that the markets across the world are still fairly segmented but are slowly becoming more integrated.

QUESTION: Is the 50-basis-points cost of hedging figure based on the experience of your firm?

CARR: Yes, it is based on the experience of our firm. To be more specific, we can break the cost down into different parts. The 50-basis-points cost is reasonable in the first year; it becomes 40 basis points in subsequent years, assuming you are rolling over the hedges every month. If you roll over the hedges every three months, the cost will be lower. Market impact costs must also be considered. It has been our experience that when relatively small amounts of money are traded in the foreign exchange markets—for example, $5 to $10 million—there is a certain cost, but spreads widen when you get up to $50 to $100 million.

Universal Hedging

Fischer Black

I have long wondered why people do not invest more abroad. In the 1970s, I told myself that it was because of barriers like withholding taxes and currency controls. But since then, different countries have eliminated withholding taxes, created exemptions, and cut out most of the currency controls. So such barriers are no longer good excuses for not investing abroad. It may simply be fear of the unknown that keeps investors out of foreign markets. Specifically, they may be afraid of foreign equity risk, foreign currency risk, or both. If currency risk is the barrier, then I wonder why they do not invest more abroad and hedge out the currency risk.

In the 1970s, I worked out the usual equilibrium model of international investment; it had no barriers to foreign investment and ignored currency factors. The optimal portfolio for everyone in that case is the world market portfolio mixed with borrowing and lending. I also looked at what happens if there are barriers to foreign investment (investment outside the home country). The barriers make investors shift away from a world market portfolio and toward more domestic stock investments.

There is one interesting feature of the model with no barriers. If you assume that everybody holds a world market portfolio, it turns out that there is a certain symmetry in the foreign holdings of different investors. The Japanese holdings of U.S. investors turn out to be equal to the U.S. holdings of Japanese investors. They have equal dollar value or equal yen value. This is true for all the pairs of countries in that kind of simple model. The holdings that investors in Country A have in Country B are equal to the holdings that investors in Country B have in Country A.

I did not think about international investment again until I began working at Goldman Sachs. The people who trade foreign stocks at Goldman typically take on their positions to accommodate clients. They do not want to hold their positions very long—a few minutes, a few days, or at most a few weeks. But even with such short-term positions, they routinely hedge out the currency risk. Curiously, the percentage that they hedge depends on the type of company they are trading: For multinationals, they hedge less than 100 percent of the currency risk; for non-multinationals, they fully hedge the risk.

Puzzled by how they decided exactly what percentage to hedge, I started to do some research on the correlations between currencies and country markets, and currencies and particular stock returns. I wanted to find a quantitative way to figure out the optimal hedge. Meanwhile, people started writing papers on currency hedging for investors who hold portfolios for the long term. These papers were written for investors who were interested in maximizing expected return for a given risk, or minimizing risk for a given expected return.

André Perold and Evan Schulman (1988) said that long-run investors might as well assume that expected returns on currency contracts are zero. They should expect to neither gain nor lose by hedging currency risk. The same argument has been used for not hedging: If you are not going to gain or lose in the long run, why bother? Perold and Schulman accepted that assumption, but nevertheless found that everyone should hedge 100 percent. If each investor measures his portfolio's expected return and risk in terms of his own currency, then each can gain by hedging 100 percent of the currency risk.

Because U.S. investors' Japanese holdings are equal to Japanese investors' U.S. holdings, investors could hedge without putting pressure on the exchange rate or on the price of the forward contract they are using to hedge. It should all match up. That is, U.S. investors could short yen against dollars in an amount equal to their Japanese holdings, and Japanese investors could short dollars against yen in an amount equal to their U.S. holdings. The two sides could be counterparties to one forward contract because the amounts would be equal. This appealed to my intuition.

I did not really believe that the expected returns on currencies are zero. My research in correlations showed that currencies sometimes have fairly strong correlations with market movements. There are two ways to interpret this: Either markets have currency risk, or currencies have market risk. So if the expected returns on various national markets are positive because people have to be paid for taking market risk, I figured that the same would apply to currencies. That is, currencies that were correlated with those national markets would have either positive or negative expected returns. Nonetheless, by using the correct expected returns on the currencies in a full equilibrium model, I thought I might get Perold and Schulman's result—that everyone should hedge 100 percent of their foreign investments.

While I was thinking about all of this, I was asked to give a talk to a group of pension plan sponsors. I chose currency hedging for my topic, and began working through the math of a general model of currency hedging. In my presentation to the plan sponsors, I explained my conclusion that hedging 100 percent was the right thing to do in an equilibrium model with no barriers to foreign investment and no barriers to currency positions.

But I was not completely satisfied with that answer. So after Christmas Day last year, I went away to a quiet place and started writing down formulas. By the Monday after Christmas I had an answer, but I thought it was wrong. I was finding that you should hedge less than 100 percent of your foreign investments. Optimistic, I started over on Tuesday morning, but got the same answer by the end of day. The same thing happened on Wednesday and Thursday. By Friday, I was convinced that I was getting the right formula, and that I had told the pension plan sponsors the wrong thing. In fact, the optimal amount of hedging kept coming out as less than 100 percent.

OPTIMAL HEDGE RATIO

In a world where everyone can hedge against changes in the value of real exchange rates (the relative values of domestic and foreign goods), and where no barriers limit international investment, there is a universal constant that tells what fraction of your foreign investments you should hedge:

$$\frac{\mu_m - \sigma_m^2}{\mu_m - \frac{1}{2}\sigma_e^2}$$

where:

μ_m is the average across investors of the expected return on the world market portfolio (over and above each investor's riskless interest rate). Here the world market portfolio contains stocks from all major countries in proportion to each country's market value;

σ_m is the average across investors of the volatility of the world market portfolio (where we average variances rather than standard deviations); and

σ_e is the average exchange rate volatility across all pairs of countries (where we average variances).

All the usual equilibrium assumptions apply: no taxes, no trading costs, and so forth.

The formula holds several surprises. First, although the model cannot distinguish long bonds from short bonds (because it is a one-period model), it says you should hedge foreign bonds 100 percent. It says that everybody holds a portfolio made up of assets that have both stock and currency risk, as well as domestic lending. You could do such lending either by lending in your own currency or by lending in a foreign currency and hedging your bonds. You could still hold foreign bonds to diversify interest-rate risk, but you would be hedging out the currency risk in those bonds, probably using short-term contracts.

The model's second surprise is that all investors should hedge their foreign stocks by the same percentage. There is an optimal percent for all pairs of an investor and his investment. U.S. investors should hedge their West German stocks by that percentage, West German investors should hedge their U.K. stocks by that percentage, and so on.

The third surprise is that this percentage is always less than 100 percent. Using my estimates for the formula's inputs, the optimal ratio turns out to be 77 percent. (An example appears in **Table 1.**) The ratio is less than 100 percent because of Siegel's paradox (Siegel 1972).

When I was at M.I.T., I told my students that Siegel's paradox is a mathematical curiosity, one that has no particular implications for investments. It is just another version of the fact that a portfolio that goes up 20 percent and then goes down 20 percent does not end up at its starting value. It is a simple mathematical fact that normally does not mean much. But in this particular case, it *does* mean something because you are evaluating your portfolio in terms of your own currency, using your own consumption good. Because the model assumes that you are dealing with real exchange-rate contracts, most of any exchange-rate change is the result of a change in the domestic consumption good's price relative to that of the foreign consumption good. Empirical evidence shows that most of the changes in exchange rates for the major industrial countries are changes in relative prices. **Table 2** shows an example of Siegel's paradox.

Siegel's paradox means that exchange-rate bets

TABLE 1. Currency Hedging Formula: Example

Sample Input Values:

μ_m	8%
σ_m	15%
σ_e	10%

$$\text{Hedge Ratio} = \frac{.08 - .15^2}{.08 - .10^2}$$

$$= 77 \text{ percent}$$

Source: Black (1989a)

are not a zero-sum game. Such bets are not zero between two countries, nor do they add up to zero when you look at the yen-dollar exchange rate and then at the dollar-yen exchange rate. They add up to more than zero. So exchange-rate bets are a positive-sum game. When investors take on currency risk, someone gains and someone loses in every period. But the gainer's gain will be greater than the loser's loss when each views his position in terms of his own currency.

Let's look at an example. Suppose we know today the yen-dollar rate is going to either double or be half of its current rate at the end of a certain period. So the dollar-yen rate is perfectly symmetrical. Let's also suppose that the chance of each of these happening is 50:50. So a dollar-based investor, looking at one unit of yen risk—for example, what he will get by holding a bond in yen—will find that he has a 50 percent chance of a 100 percent gain, measuring his returns in dollars, and a 50 percent chance of a 50 percent loss. The expected gain from one unit of yen risk is 25 percent—it is positive. It looks the same from the point of view of the yen investor who takes one unit of dollar risk. He, too, has a 50 percent chance of a 100 percent gain and a 50 percent chance of a 50 percent loss. So his expected return from taking one unit of dollar risk is 25 percent, too. Therefore, both investors would be better off not fully hedging their currency risk. Instead they can take on some of the other currency's risk to increase their expected return. In short, taking on currency risk usually increases risk measured in your own currency, but it pays to take on a little bit of foreign currency risk. Over time, the extra risk will pay off and you will have an optimal mix of currency risk and stock risk.

TABLE 2. Siegel's Paradox

Quarter	Start-of-Quarter Exchange Rates: Mark/Dollar	Start-of-Quarter Exchange Rates: Dollar/Mark	Percentage Changes in Exchange Rates: Mark/Dollar	Percentage Changes in Exchange Rates: Dollar/Mark
1Q 84	2.75	0.362	-5.58	5.90
2Q 84	2.60	0.384	7.18	-6.69
3Q 84	2.79	0.358	9.64	-8.79
4Q 84	3.06	0.326	3.66	-3.52
1Q 85	3.17	0.315	-1.83	1.84
2Q 85	3.11	0.321	-2.25	2.30
3Q 85	3.04	0.328	-13.04	15.01
4Q 85	2.64	0.377	-7.59	8.21
1Q 86	2.44	0.408	-4.46	4.67
2Q 86	2.33	0.427	-6.80	7.29
3Q 86	2.17	0.459	-7.16	7.73
4Q 86	2.02	0.494	-5.19	5.46
1Q 87	1.91	0.521	-5.11	5.41
2Q 87	1.81	0.549	0.49	-0.49
3Q 87	1.82	0.547	1.09	-1.08
4Q 87	1.84	0.541	-14.00	16.28
1Q 88	1.58	0.629	4.29	-4.12
2Q 88	1.65	0.603	9.83	-8.95
3Q 88	1.82	0.549	2.27	-2.22
4Q 88	1.86	0.537	-4.88	5.12
Average			-1.97	2.47

Source: Black (1989b)

The formula for the optimal fraction to hedge held other surprises too. For example, it depends on three broad averages. First, there is an average of the extra amount you get from holding stocks over holding bonds—the weighted average risk premium across currencies. It is the extra amount that you get on average from stocks over bonds. The second is the average stock volatility of the whole world market portfolio from the viewpoint of different currencies. The third is the average exchange-rate volatility, averaged across all pairs of countries. For both the stock volatilities and the exchange-rate volatilities, we are averaging the variances rather than the standard deviations.

The formula's missing variables are also interesting. For example, the equilibrium expected currency changes do not appear, so it does not matter whether they are zero. Similarly, I do not assume that the currency changes are independent of stock market moves, nor do I assume that they are independent of each other. Nonetheless, correlations between currency movements and stock movements, or between one currency movement and another, do not appear in the formula. I have decided that these two things cancel. In other words, think of the correlations and expected returns as being in the formula, but just cancelling one another. The simple option-pricing model is similar: Neither the stock's expected return nor its beta affect the option formula, because the two cancel each other.

CONCLUSION

Currency hedging does not always reduce risk. The correlations may be such that putting on a hedge does not reduce the risk of a particular investment, but it does increase the expected return. On the other side of the transaction, an investor will pay you to take the opposing position because it reduces his risk. So it ends up that you put on the same hedge no matter where you are, either because it reduces your risk, increases your expected return, or provides some combination of the two.

Of course, all of this depends on the notion that the world is in equilibrium. In a practical situation, if you have particular views on currencies, you might vary the amount of hedging you do above or below the amount suggested by this formula. Think of the formula as a base case, a position that an investor would normally hold over the long run.

Question and Answer Session

QUESTION: Does the non-zero-sum game depend entirely on Siegel's paradox?

BLACK: I think it does. If the Siegel's paradox effect is not assumed, then I think you will get the Perold-Schulman result that everyone should hedge 100 percent of their foreign investment risk.

QUESTION: Does Siegel's paradox depend on the mathematical principle that no one revises expectations in the light of actual events?

BLACK: No, it does not depend on people having incorrect expectations of currency changes. It is there when everybody has absolutely rational expectations.

QUESTION: If the non-zero-sum game is dependent on Siegel's paradox, then presumably the wider the diversity of opinion, the more everyone benefits. Does your model imply that investors' utility would increase if each state in the United States had its own currency?

BLACK: There is nothing specifically international in this model, so if there were a way for people to hedge the changes in relative value of consumption in Boston and consumption in New York, or Boston versus San Francisco, then people would gain by putting on positions like that. Those changes are probably not as significant as the changes between the United States and other countries, so you would not gain as much. But in principle there would be gains.

QUESTION: Please expand on the assumptions. Does the result depend on the symmetry assumption between domestic and foreign investors? Do the investment markets in each country have to be the same size? Do investors have to have the same market expectations and aversions to risk?

BLACK: The main assumption is that everybody shares the same information and that the numbers are all calculated correctly. Therefore, everyone should have the same expectations for various quantities in the model—for example, the same expectations about the change in the dollar-yen rate. There is no symmetry assumption. Investors can differ in wealth and their risk tolerance.

QUESTION: Under what conditions would the optimal hedge be zero?

BLACK: Technically, the optimal hedge would be zero if everyone had log utility. It does not have to be always above zero; it could even be negative. If you are the other side of log utility, then it will be negative.

QUESTION: Please elaborate on why 77 percent is the right number, and why it is the same for everybody.

BLACK: I have no intuition about why 77 is the right number. Investors are paid for taking stock risk. Because of Siegel's paradox, investors are also paid, on average, for taking exchange risk. Therefore, there is an optional mix of those two risks, and it turns out that the optimal mix of those two risks is the same for everybody, no matter where they are. That is why you have the same percentage hedging for everybody.

QUESTION: Please elaborate on why one would have 100 percent hedging in foreign bonds.

BLACK: You will hedge your foreign bonds 100 percent if you buy them for diversification reasons. Mixing domestic and foreign bonds can help you diversify your interest rate risk. On the other hand, if you buy foreign bonds because you think the currency will appreciate, you should not hedge them at all. Finally, if you buy foreign bonds because they have high yields, you may or may not want to hedge them. If hedging takes away the yield advantage, you won't want to do it.

QUESTION: Would it be accurate to say that if an investor is risk-neutral across all markets with respect to currency exposure, then 100 percent hedging is appropriate in the context of Siegel's paradox?

BLACK: Risk-neutrality is a troublesome concept, because it means that you will take any amount of risk as long as you can increase your expected return. This usually means investors will take huge amounts of stock risk and huge amounts of exchange risk, which in turn requires that they borrow to buy stocks and have to put on reverse hedges in foreign currencies to continue to increase their expected return. As people generally become more risk tolerant, they will hedge less and less, because stock risk will become less attractive than currency risk. So the appropriate amount of hedging goes to zero, or may even be negative.

QUESTION: Can we assume that, over the long run, the premium or discount on forward contracts for hedging will equal the currency return?

BLACK: The empirical evidence on this is mixed. I have assumed that when an interest rate is high, it reflects expected depreciation in that country's currency. In fact, in the period since currencies were allowed to float, you would have gained by investing in high-interest-rate currencies. You would not have lost as much from depreciation as you would think from the differences in the interest rate. I think that is unlikely to continue.

QUESTION: In your example, the changes in currency movements are not symmetric—they were up 100 percent or down 50 percent. If the changes were symmetric, would that have affected Siegel's paradox?

BLACK: You can never make the paradox go away. For example, the yen can go up 20 percent or down 20 percent relative to the dollar. But then when you turn that around and look at what it means for the dollar relative to the yen, that expected change is then positive. If its zero from one side, it will be positive from the other side.

Hedging a Non-Dollar Fixed-Income Portfolio

Michael Rosenberg

The presentations in these proceedings address two distinct issues: separating the currency and asset decision on a tactical basis and the notion that a free lunch is available by passively hedging a foreign portfolio (although this has not been stated explicitly). There have been a number of articles on this subject; the work by Perold and Schulman in the *Financial Analysts Journal* (Perold and Schulman 1988) has received considerable attention. The authors of several articles have argued that, by hedging currency, one can reduce portfolio risk without sacrificing return. I strongly disagree with this argument.

In this presentation, I will show that currency hedging offers no free lunch. Currency hedging should be used as a tactical tool to manage currency risk actively in a global portfolio of either stocks or bonds. In fact, I am going to show that a passively managed, hedged foreign bond portfolio is actually more expensive than one that is not hedged.

THE FREE LUNCH DEBATE

The evidence on risk and return of international bond diversification shows that only a modest reduction in portfolio risk may be achieved through traditional, unhedged international diversification, largely because of currency volatility. Currency hedging separates and removes the currency risk (volatility associated with international bond investment). Therefore, if we eliminate that currency volatility, always-hedged foreign bonds should be less volatile than comparable unhedged foreign bonds in U.S. dollar terms. Further, it has been argued that currency hedging should involve no loss of return if no risk premium is embedded in forward exchange rates. So far, this is all fairly straightforward and all true. **Figure 1** shows that hedged foreign bonds dominate unhedged foreign bonds, if looked at singularly. In other words, for a given level of expected return, hedged foreign bonds have less risk. Therefore, according to this argument, there is a free lunch in currency hedging. Always-hedged foreign bonds offer greater risk reduction with no loss of expected return than that available from traditional unhedged international diversification. If you wish to own non-dollar bonds, you can have less risk with the same level of return, as the advocates of currency hedging have been arguing.

My counter-argument to the free lunch view is that in the long run it makes no difference whether a foreign bond portfolio is hedged or not. The same diversification benefits will result, assuming no transaction costs. If we assume there are transaction costs and other fees associated with hedging, always hedging results in a more expensive lunch than if you never hedged at all.

The whole free lunch argument has come about because, historically, a free lunch was available in owning hedged foreign bonds. **Figure 2** shows the risk-return trade-offs of having a portfolio of U.S. domestic bonds versus hedged and unhedged non-dollar bonds. Only a modest reduction in portfolio risk could have been achieved through unhedged diversification. Through hedged diversification, however, the historical evidence shows that we would not have sacrificed anything in total return, and a dramatic reduction in portfolio risk would have resulted had we bought a portfolio of hedged foreign bonds and included it with U.S. bonds. In fact, the evidence shows that we should not have owned any U.S. bonds in our portfolio; we should have owned a portfolio of only hedged non-dollar bonds.

This conclusion is reached because non-dollar bonds have been much less volatile than U.S. bonds historically. One reason for this lower volatility involves institutional factors. The U.S. market had been liberalized more than the overseas markets. For example, major capital flow restrictions were in effect in the United Kingdom and Japan, and the development of futures and options markets has advanced much more quickly in the U.S. market than in the overseas markets. As a result, overseas markets have operated under an inherent inability to generate much volatility.

A second reason why foreign markets have been less volatile involves macroeconomic policies. Over the past 10 years, the United States has pursued more unstable policies than either West Germany or Japan. In the past, the foreign markets were less volatile

FIGURE 1. Hedged Foreign Bonds Dominate Unhedged Foreign Bonds

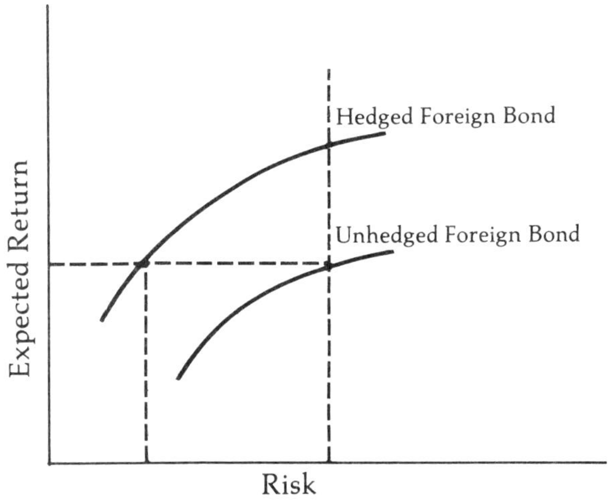

Source: Merrill Lynch

than the U.S. market. Today, however, we have to ask whether there is any reason why the foreign bond markets should be less volatile in the future. If it could be guaranteed that foreign bond markets will continue to be less volatile than the U.S. bond market in the future, I would concur with the view that there is a free lunch in hedged foreign bonds. If there is an innate structural reason why hedged foreign bonds are less volatile than U.S. bonds, they would constitute a unique asset class, just as cash is a unique asset class because of its lower volatility. However, if foreign bonds cannot be guaranteed to have the same volatility as U.S. bonds, then hedged foreign bonds offer no special benefits.

If hedged foreign bonds really provide a free lunch, they should provide a free lunch not just to U.S. investors but to all investors. In pursuing this idea, I examined the historical evidence from a Japanese investor's perspective to see whether he also enjoyed a free lunch. The evidence shows that the Japanese investor actually had a very, very expensive lunch. In terms of both risk and return, the yen-based investor would have been much better off owning his own market alone. Yen bonds had much higher returns and much less risk than either hedged or unhedged non-yen bonds. Had the Japanese investor created a portfolio of hedged and unhedged foreign bonds, he could have reduced his risk somewhat, but he would have had to sacrifice return to get that risk reduction. In addition, the amount of risk reduction was fairly small; in fact, the yen-based investor would have obtained more risk reduction by having unhedged non-yen bonds than by owning

FIGURE 2. Historical Risk-Return Trade-off: U.S. Domestic Bonds Versus Hedged and Unhedged Non-dollar Bonds 1978-88 (Annualized Monthly Returns and Standard Deviations)

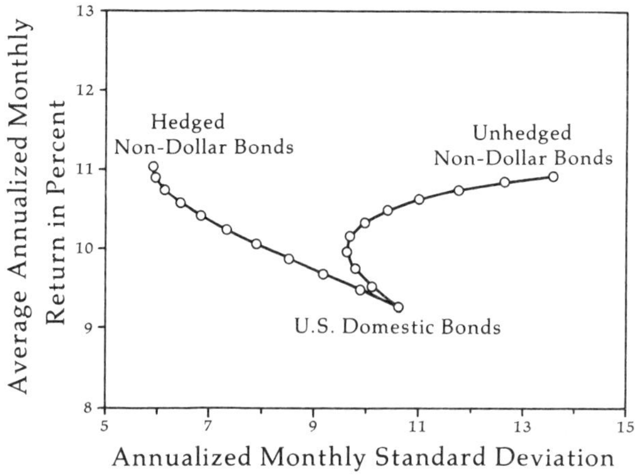

Source: Merrill Lynch

hedged non-yen bonds. The historical risk-return trade-off of yen bonds versus hedged and unhedged non-yen bonds is shown in **Figure 3**.

FIGURE 3. Historical Risk-Return Trade-off: Yen Bonds Versus Hedged and Unhedged Non-Yen Bonds 1978-88 (Annualized Monthly Returns and Standard Deviations)

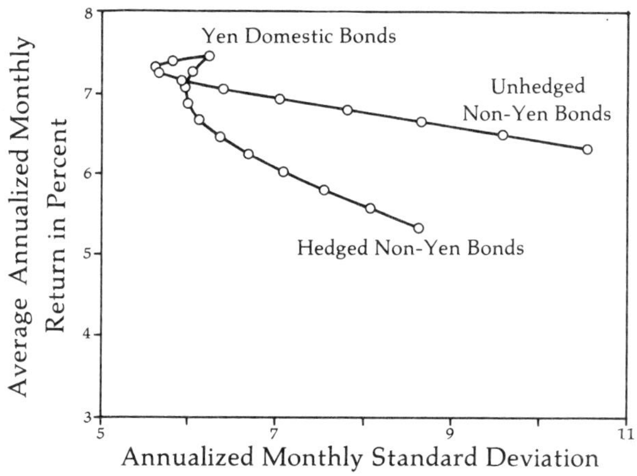

Source: Merrill Lynch

Most investors agree that expected returns across markets should be the same, whether hedged or unhedged and versus the U.S. market, but we still debate whether expected volatilities should be the same or different. I believe we will see, over the coming years, a greater convergence of global bond market volatilities. As a result of financial liberalization, deregulation, and the introduction of futures and options in many of the overseas bond markets, there is going to be much greater volatility in these markets.

Further, with the converging of world inflation rates and of macroeconomic policies, there is no reason why U.S. economic policy will be more volatile than foreign economic policy in the next 10 years. We cannot guarantee with any degree of precision, therefore, that foreign bond markets will be any less volatile than U.S. bonds. In fact, the convergence is already starting. **Table 1** shows foreign bond market volatilities from 1983 to 1988 for the United States, Japan, and West Germany. In 1983, the U.S. bond market had nearly twice as much volatility as the German and Japanese markets. By 1985, a futures contract on JGBs was introduced in Tokyo. In three of the four years from 1985 to 1988, the Japanese bond market either had equal or greater volatility than the U.S. bond market. West Germany is still lagging, but this is because a futures market was introduced—not in West Germany, but on the London futures exchange—only last September. I suspect that as we move closer to Europe in 1992 and to a more eclectic European monetary policy, and as we shift from a Bundesbank standard to a more eclectic standard in macroeconomic policy in Europe, we will see the volatilities converging, not just between the United States and Japan, but between the United States, Japan, and West Germany as well.

In addition to this volatility consideration, currency-hedged foreign bonds are not as efficient a diversifier as unhedged foreign bonds. Currency volatility may add to the total volatility of a foreign bond, but currency volatility also helps to reduce the co-movement between U.S. and foreign bonds. **Table 2** shows the correlation of U.S. bonds with hedged foreign bonds and unhedged foreign bonds. The monthly data indicate that there is a lower correlation between U.S. and unhedged foreign bonds than there is between U.S. and hedged foreign bonds. In other words, unhedged foreign bonds are a more efficient diversifier than hedged foreign bonds. Quarterly data indicate much stronger correlations between U.S. and foreign bonds, either hedged or unhedged, but with a correlation of 0.82, hedged foreign bonds are increasingly becoming a very close substitute for U.S. bonds.

Let me present a simple exercise to illustrate the proper way to view currency-hedged foreign bonds. Historically, the United States has had a 9.3 percent average return over the past 10 years. Let us assume that this represents the expected return on U.S. bonds in the future. Let us further assume that this return is the same for hedged non-dollar and unhedged non-dollar bonds, an assumption almost everyone would agree with. Table 3 presents the theoretical expected return and expected standard deviation values used in the example. I am now going to argue that the volatility of hedged non-dollar bonds will match the U.S. historical standard deviation of 10.62. This is very different from the claim that the expected volatility of foreign bonds will be equal to their past volatility, which was substantially lower than the U.S. historic volatility. This is a critical assumption: in other studies it is assumed that hedged non-dollar volatilities are closer to 5 percent than to the 10.6 percent estimate. Unhedged non-dollar bond volatility is assumed to equal its historic average of 13.57 percent. **Table 3** shows that the U.S., hedged non-dollar, and unhedged non-dollar bonds all have the same expected return.

Figure 4 illustrates what we get when we combine a portfolio of U.S. domestic bonds with hedged non-dollar bonds and with unhedged non-dollar bonds. Combining U.S. domestic bonds and hedged non-dollar bonds reduces overall portfolio risk without sacrificing return. Combining U.S. domestic bonds and unhedged non-dollar bonds produces the same minimum risk portfolio. Why? Although hedged foreign bonds are less volatile than unhedged foreign bonds, unhedged foreign bonds are a more efficient diversifier,

TABLE 1. Convergence of U.S. and Foreign Bond Market Volatilities

	U.S.	*Japan*	*West Germany*
1983	8.2	3.8	4.7
1984	9.3	3.3	3.7
1985	8.5	9.2	5.3
1986	9.3	6.6	6.2
1987	11.8	16.1	6.8
1988	6.9	6.3	4.2

Source: Merrill Lynch

TABLE 2. The Diversification Benefit of Currency Risk

	Correlation of U.S. Bonds With:	
	Hedged Foreign Bonds	*Unhedged Foreign Bonds*
Monthly data	0.54	0.42
Quarterly data	0.82	0.62

Source: Merrill Lynch; Ennis, Knupp & Assoc.

TABLE 3. Theoretical Long-run Averages

	Expected Return	*Expected Standard Deviation*	*Correlation With U.S. Bonds*
U.S. domestic bonds	9.3*	10.62*	1.00*
Hedged non-dollar bonds	9.3	10.62	0.54*
Unhedged non-dollar bonds	9.3	13.57*	0.42*

* Historic average

Source: Merrill Lynch

because the lower correlation between U.S. bonds and unhedged foreign bonds overcomes the fact that they are more volatile. The diversification benefits of U.S. bonds and hedged non-dollar bonds result from the somewhat lower volatility of hedged bonds. **Figure 5** illustrates the theoretical diversification benefits from portfolio combinations of U.S. bonds and hedged/unhedged foreign bonds. So, it really does not matter whether you combine U.S. bonds with hedged foreign bonds or unhedged foreign bonds. Indeed, there is no free lunch in currency hedging.

This leads to what I term Rosenberg Proposition Number 1: In a world free of transaction costs, the amount of risk reduction available from international diversification in the long run is independent of whether the currency risk is hedged or not. Those of you who follow finance theory will recognize this as a variation on the Modigliani-Miller proposition that the value of the firm is independent of its capital structure, meaning it is independent of its debt-equity mix.

Unfortunately, the story does not end here. As Richard Carr discussed earlier, there are extra costs

FIGURE 4. Theoretical Long-run Expected Return and Risk on U.S. Domestic, Hedged Non-dollar, and Unhedged Non-dollar Bonds

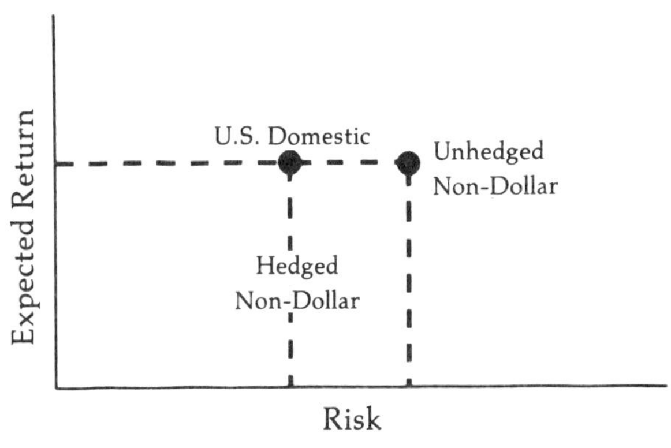

Source: Merrill Lynch

FIGURE 5. Theoretical Diversification Benefits From Portfolio Combinations of U.S. and Hedged/Unhedged Foreign Bonds

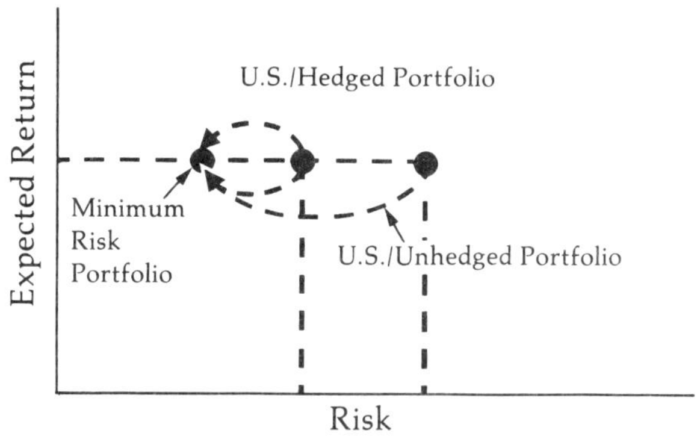

Source: Merrill Lynch

associated with a passively managed hedged portfolio that are not associated with a passively managed unhedged portfolio.[1] These costs are of three types: greater execution costs in terms of bid-offer spreads; settlement costs, custodial fees, greater in-house operation costs associated with monitoring and tracking the rolling hedges; and greater management fees, because a passively managed hedged portfolio involves more work. **Table 4** presents an estimate of the range of transaction costs for each category. This additional cost is estimated to be between 27 and 60 basis points. Richard Carr estimated the extra cost at 40 to 50 basis points.

If, instead of a no-transaction-cost world where the expected returns are the same, we assume there are transaction costs that cause the expected return on a hedged portfolio to be reduced, we arrive at Rosenberg Proposition Number 2: In a world where transaction costs and management fees are not insignificant, hedged foreign bonds will be a more expensive route to achieve risk reduction through international diversification. Instead of this strategy being a free lunch, it ends up being a more expensive lunch.

There are several implications of this finding for pension plan sponsors and portfolio managers. First, it makes no difference whether a portfolio's foreign currency exposure is hedged. Second, contrary to what some advocates propose, hedged foreign bonds should not be accorded special status as a separate asset class, because they offer no added value. Third, because the same minimum-risk

[1]See Mr. Carr's presentation, pp. 22-27.

TABLE 4. **Transaction Costs Associated With Managing a Hedged Foreign Bond Portfolio**

	Basis Points
Execution costs	12 - 25
Settlement costs	5 - 25
Management fees	10
Total	27 - 60

Source: Ennis, Knupp & Assoc.

portfolio will be obtained whether you are hedged or unhedged, it is largely irrelevant whether you use a hedged or an unhedged benchmark to evaluate your total return performance.

NEED TO REFOCUS DEBATE

I think the whole debate over global fixed-income management needs to be redirected. The debate has really been about risk reduction. When we could not get risk reduction, we debated about separating the currency and asset decisions and trying to find some evidence that a policy of always hedging provided a free lunch. In the end, however, I think the evidence indicates the amount of risk reduction available from international investing, whether hedged or unhedged, is fairly limited.

The real benefits of international diversification come from active management, not from risk reduction. By broadening one's investment horizon to all the different markets, and taking an active management posture, international investing provides substantial opportunities to enhance portfolio return. In fact, when we look at the historical evidence, on average, the difference between the best- and worst-performing markets around the world is 35 to 40 percentage points—that is, 3,500 to 4,000 basis points. The difference between the U.S. and the best-performing markets each year averages nearly 1,200 to 1,500 basis points. **Figure 6** illustrates the total return performances of the best, worst, and U.S. outcomes from 1973 to 1988.

CONCLUSION

The whole international investment game is going to change over the next five to ten years. Until now, dedicated international bond managers have been trying to promote non-dollar bonds as a separate asset class for U.S. pension plans. That is going to change. In the next five to ten years, instead of dedicated non-dollar managers, there will be broad-based U.S. managers offering investments in

FIGURE 6. **Total Return Performances of the Best, Worst, and U.S. Outcomes**

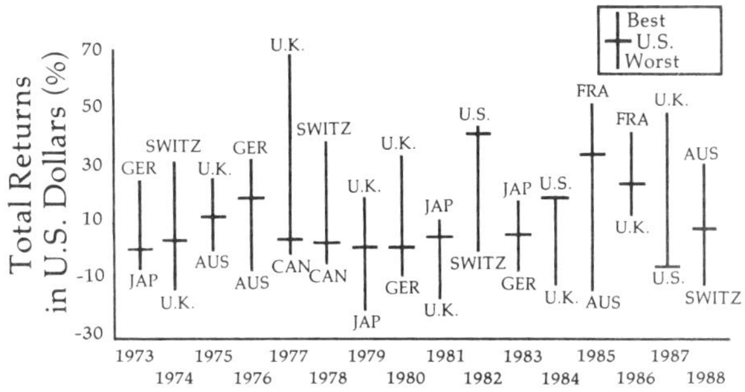

Source: Merrill Lynch

many areas—government bonds, corporate bonds, mortgages, and non-dollar bonds. There really is only one fixed-income asset class (bonds), not two (U.S. and foreign). Ultimately, the decision between domestic and foreign bonds will become a broad strategic decision. **Figure 7** illustrates a model of tactical global asset allocation for bonds. Each pension plan and portfolio manager will make this decision based on his view of currency and interest-rate trends, how much he wants to be in domestic bonds, and how much he wants to be in foreign bonds. So there is really only one fixed-income asset class decision—how much to put in bonds; the hedging decision is only a tactical decision.

Hedging should be done as part of an overall active management stance. Always hedging foreign bonds and always hedging the currency risk offers no free lunch. I am not saying that hedging should not be done; I am arguing that it should not be done passively.

FIGURE 7. **Tactical Global Asset Allocation**

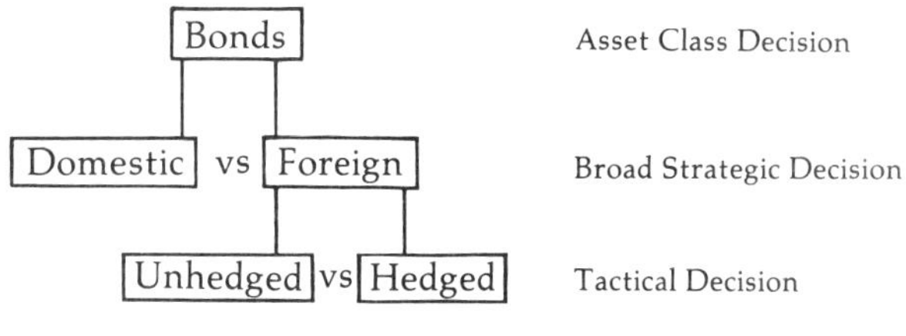

Source: Merrill Lynch

Question and Answer Session

QUESTION: Are U.S. investors in an unfavorable position because the dollar is the international currency? How would this affect a West German investor?

ROSENBERG: The United States used to be the benchmark, the numeraire, but I think we are going to move steadily, over time, to a three-country reserve currency system. Although I would argue that the West German investor is getting a double whammy on the up side in the U.S. market this year, he is also getting a bond rally and a currency rally.

QUESTION: Your main contention has been that hedging is irrelevant over the long term. How long is the long term?

ROSENBERG: I think 10- to 15-year returns and standard deviations are standard periods for evaluating portfolios. If you are going to conduct these studies fairly, however, you cannot use historical data on volatility. Historically, volatilities have been inordinately influenced by certain macroeconomic policies in the United States and by certain institutional rigidities overseas, which are now being eliminated.

QUESTION: Why should the existence of futures and options trading and markets lead to increases in volatility in the instruments?

ROSENBERG: In Japan, we have seen a much sharper rise in volatility, probably because investors who did not have to manage actively are forced to manage more actively as greater freedoms are introduced into that market. Investors are still much less active in West Germany, and there is less volatility.

QUESTION: Would your conclusions about the risk-return trade-off for yen bonds change if you used a different time period?

ROSENBERG: The past 10 years of data represent a period when Japan was under certain institutional rigidities that contributed to a very stable bond market. Until the last three years, it would not matter whether you were looking at an up or down movement in the yen or the yen bond market, because it was fairly stable. Over the past three years, both in a strong and a weak yen environment, we have seen much greater volatility in that market.

QUESTION: Did the Louvre Accord bias data?

ROSENBERG: Since the Louvre Accord of February 1987, currency volatility has been sharply reduced, although that might have changed this year. At the same time, there has been a sharp reduction in U.S. bond market volatility. The convergence in bond market volatilities is attributable in part to the rise in volatility in Japan, but also to the reduction in U.S. bond market volatility, which is probably related to the fact that the United States is now pursuing much more stable monetary policies.

QUESTION: Does your long-term perspective imply investors should only hold stocks, no bonds?

ROSENBERG: No. Although stocks will outperform bonds in the long run, the inclusion of bonds in a broadly diversified portfolio does contribute to a meaningful reduction in portfolio risk. What I have tried to argue is that you should not expect to see any greater reduction in portfolio risk by adopting a policy of always being helged against currency risk.

Hedging Opportunities

Mark P. Kritzman, CFA

There are two basic aspects of currency management: hedging currency exposure to minimize risk and managing currency exposure to add value. I am going to concentrate on managing currency exposure to add value. Before I do that, I would like to make a couple of observations about the issue of hedging.

THE HEDGING DECISION

It is not particularly useful to rely on historical precedent to determine whether hedging is a good idea, because it is always possible to find a period where hedging would have benefitted a portfolio and another period where it would have hurt a portfolio. Instead, one should take a forward perspective. There are three considerations that determine the desirability of hedging: (1) the currency's expected return, (2) the currency's risk, and (3) the currency's hedging effectiveness.

The optimal hedge ratio depends on the correlation between the currency and the assets. To illustrate this notion, consider two assets, one domestic asset and one foreign asset, that have the same expected return and the same standard deviation. The currency is assumed to have a zero expected return. The currency return is calculated as the percentage change from the forward rate to the spot rate at expiration. By defining return this way, currency is really the asset that will be in your portfolio; it is the instrument that will be traded. A lot of the arithmetic in the optimal hedging formulas drops out, because the dynamics of the interest-rate differentials are subsumed in the estimates of the parameters.

The best way to think about hedging is to separate the foreign asset return into two components: the currency return and the foreign asset's local return. One might expect that there would be a positive correlation between the foreign asset return and the currency return, because the currency return is part of the foreign asset's return. There are some situations in which you do not want to hedge away the currency return, because it has diversification properties. For example, if the correlation is not very high (close to zero), the currency return is actually hedging, because it is uncorrelated with the local return of that foreign asset. **Figure 1** shows that when the correlation between the foreign asset and foreign exchange is 100 percent, the minimum risk portfolio occurs when the embedded currency exposure of the foreign asset is 100 percent hedged. You can also contrive a situation in which the optimal hedge ratio is a situation in which you are fully exposed to the currency (see **Figure 2**).

The typical situation is one in which you are not at either extreme, and there is an optimal hedge ratio that is somewhere between zero and 100. **Figure 3** illustrates the risk-versus-percent-hedged frontier when the correlation is 60 percent. You can determine the optimal hedge ratio with simple algorithms. To do this, you need a simple objective function such as maximizing the portfolio's expected return, minus some risk aversion parameter times portfolio risk. In this case, I have made an assumption that there is an underlying portfolio of investments that has been arrived at independently of the currency decision. That may not be the optimal way to approach the problem, but it is typical. You also should add the constraint that you cannot be net long or short the currency; you can be as far as fully hedged or fully exposed, but you cannot go beyond those extremes.

With these simple constraints, it is easy to calculate the optimal hedge ratio by measuring the sensitivity of this objective function to the currency weight. Through an iterative procedure, the currency exposure is varied until all of the sensitivities equal zero or until you have come up against one of your constraints. That will give you the optimal solution.

ADDING VALUE THROUGH CURRENCIES

There are opportunities to make money from currencies. I am going to describe why the opportunity exists, provide evidence that the opportunity exists, and describe a very simple strategy for taking advantage of the opportunity.

The opportunity to make money with currencies exists because central banks induce nonrandomness in currency returns by intervening in foreign exchange markets to stabilize exchange rates. Nonrandom returns mean that there is predictability in currency returns. Pick up any major newspaper, for example *The New York Times* or *The Wall Street Journal*,

FIGURE 1. Optimal Hedge Ratio: 100 Percent Correlation

	Expected Return (%)	Standard Deviation(%)	Correlation U.S. Asset	Correlation Foreign Asset
U.S. Asset	10	20		
Foreign Asset	10	20	0.00	
Foreign Exchange	0	20	0.00	1.00

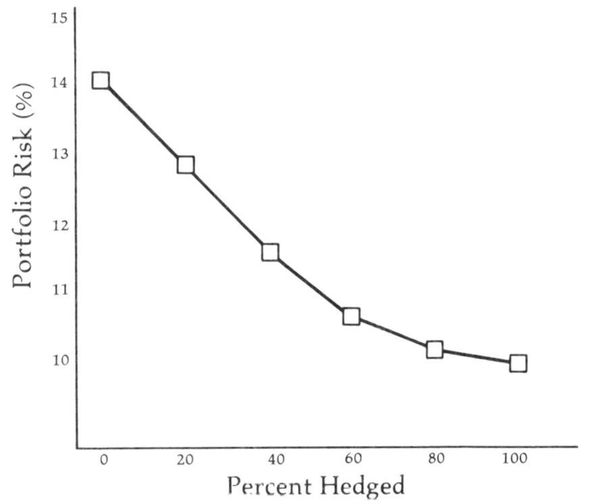

Source: Windham Capital Management

FIGURE 2. Optimal Hedge Ratio: Zero Percent Correlation

	Expected Return (%)	Standard Deviation(%)	Correlation U.S. Asset	Correlation Foreign Asset
U.S. Asset	10	20		
Foreign Asset	10	20	0.00	
Foreign Exchange	0	20	0.00	0.00

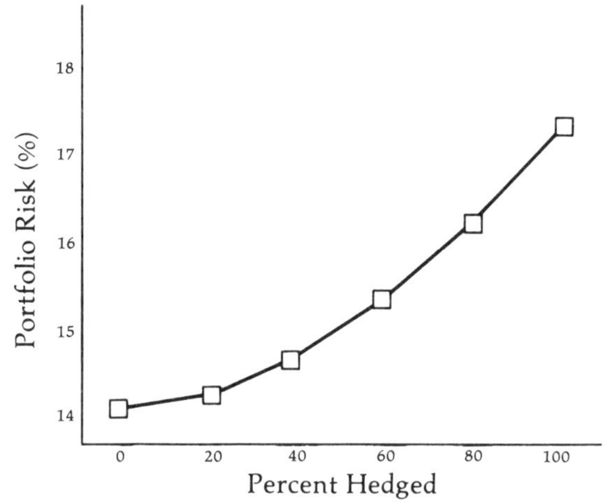

Source: Windham Capital Management

and you can find plenty of anecdotal evidence that central banks tend to provide liquidity whenever there are shocks in exchange rates. Central banks do not like abrupt movements. They like things to adjust slowly, because if the adjustment is too abrupt, instability is introduced in foreign trade in the global financial markets. So if a currency is under a lot of pressure, they will buy that currency to ease the pressure. They do not necessarily prevent the currency from eventually arriving at its new equilibrium value; they merely cushion its movement.

Think about what companies do in terms of managing dividends. Typically, if earnings rise sharply, companies will lower the payout ratio; if earnings fall sharply, they raise the payout ratio. So a time series of dividends behaves almost like a moving average of earnings. My thesis is that observed exchange rates behave as if they are a moving average of the equilibrium exchange rates—the unobservable equilibrium exchange rates—that would be obtained in the absence of central bank intervention. That provides an investment opportunity. A moving average is correlated with itself; it is positively, serially correlated. It is not random.

There is considerable empirical evidence of this nonrandomness. **Table 1** shows the results of a "runs test" on five currencies. A run is an uninterrupted sequence of either positive or negative returns in a series of returns (assuming the average return equals zero). A run is every occurrence, or series of occurrences in a row, of one outcome. A sequence of a positive return, a negative return, a positive return, and a negative return would be four runs. There is an expected number of runs from a random time series. If there are more runs than you would expect from a random sequence, that implies there is a negative serial correlation, e.g., lots of reversals (a mean-reverting process).

Alternatively, you can have fewer runs than expected by randomness. This is the case with

TABLE 1. Results of Runs Test (January 1977 to December 1988)

	Expected Number of Runs	*Actual Number of Runs*	*t-Statistic*
British Pound	73	50	-3.84
West German Mark	72	57	-2.59
Japanese Yen	73	66	-1.15
Swiss Franc	73	57	-2.63
French Franc	73	54	-2.93

Source: Windham Capital Management

currencies, as shown in Table 1. The average or the typical run is much longer than what you would get in a random series for the five currencies tested. Table 1 shows the expected number of runs for the five major currencies, the actual number of runs, and the t-statistics. For all of the currencies except the yen, there are significantly fewer runs than one would get if currency returns were random through time. This evidence is consistent with my central bank premise.

Another test for nonrandomness is what is called a variance ratio test, which I think was first proposed in the 1950s by the physicist Maury Osborne; it has become a popular test of nonrandomness in stock market returns. If a time series is random, the variance estimated from quarterly returns should be three times as large as the variance estimated from monthly returns. The variance ratio is normalized by dividing it by the number of months in the numerator. For example, if you looked at six-month intervals compared to one-month intervals, you would divide by six. So if you observe a variance ratio that is greater than one, that implies positive serial correlation. If it is less than one, you have negative serial correlation, or a mean-reverting process.

Figure 4 shows the variance ratios comparing 3-month, 6-month, 12-month, 24-month, and 36-month intervals to variances estimated from 1-month observations. All of the variance ratios are greater than one. They tend to peak around two years. The solid lines are the levels required for significance at the 5 percent level. This is evidence that variances are not linear with respect to time, as they would be if the series were random. If currency options are priced according to the assumption that variances are linear with respect to time, there are opportunities to make money here.

I will describe a trading strategy that can exploit this nonrandomness. I must attribute some of these notions to André Perold and William Sharpe (1988). If a data series has a positive serial correlation, a strategy that induces a convex payoff function will add value to a buy-and-hold strategy. This strategy will take advantage of the times when values diverge from the trend. If, on the other hand, a data series exhibits negative serial correlation, or a mean-reverting process, then a strategy that induces a concave payoff function will add value to a buy-and-hold strategy. **Figures 5 and 6** illustrate this. So one could follow a trading rule that tilts a portfolio's exposure toward a currency as it appreciates and away from the currency as it depreciates; that will induce convexity. This strategy should make money for you.

There is an implicit timing forecast in this type

FIGURE 3. Optimal Hedge Ratio: 60 Percent Correlation

	Expected Return (%)	Standard Deviation(%)	Correlation U.S. Asset	Correlation Foreign Asset
U.S. Asset	10	20		
Foreign Asset	10	20	0.00	
Foreign Exchange	0	20	0.00	0.60

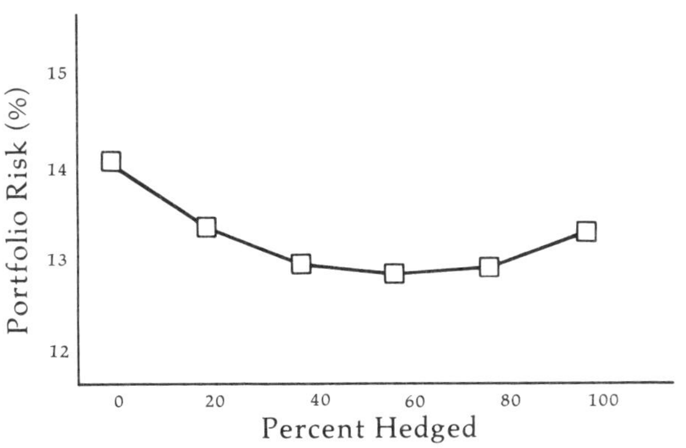

Source: Windham Capital Management

FIGURE 4. Variance Ratio Test (January 1977 to December 1988)

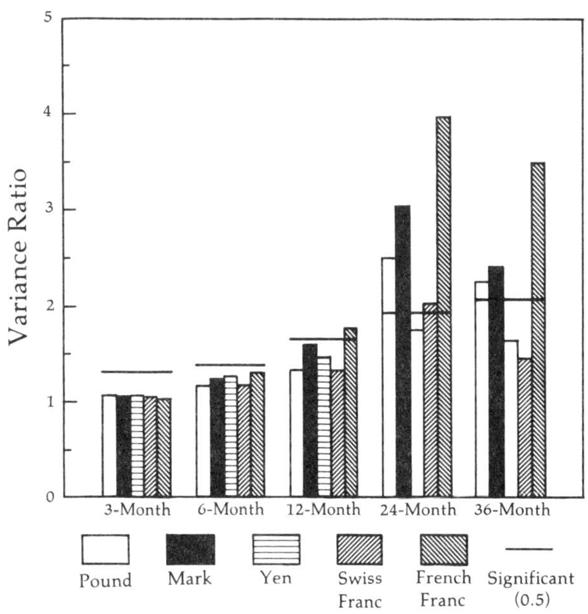

Source: Windham Capital Management

FIGURE 5. Convex Versus Buy-and-Hold

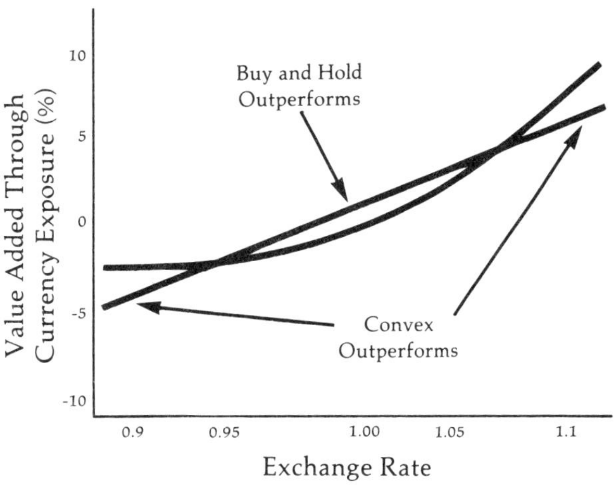

Source: Windham Capital Management

FIGURE 6. Concave Versus Buy-and-Hold

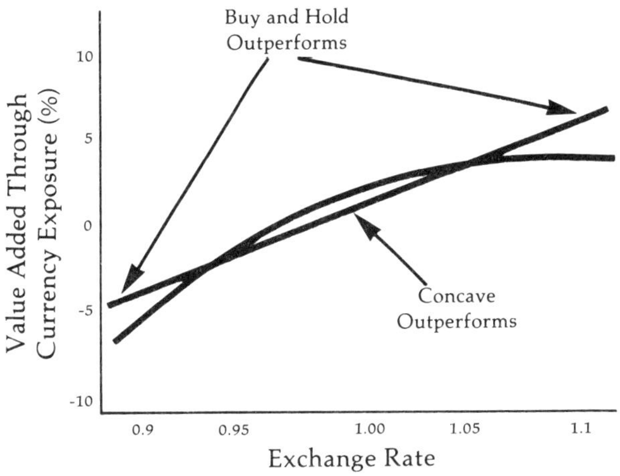

Source: Windham Capital Management

of strategy. It is based on the idea that last period's currency return predicts the direction of this period's currency return. In 1981, Bob Merton proposed a test to evaluate market-timing skill (Merton 1981). I have applied that test to this implicit timing signal from this strategy. Merton's measure of timing skill compares the number of times a market timer is correct to the expected value. For example, if stocks outperform bonds 70 percent of the time, you would compute the percentage of times you are correct when stocks do better than bonds, and the percentage of times you are correct when stocks do worse than bonds. If you have no skill at all, those numbers will sum to one, because the timer was right 100 percent of the time when stocks were better than bonds and zero percent of the time when they underperformed bonds. If you have perfect skill, that will sum to two. So anything between one and two is evidence of some skill.

Table 2 shows the results of this measure applied to the implicit forecast in my strategy that says last month's currency return forecasts the direction of this month's currency return. In four of five currencies, the confidence level is 99 percent, except for the yen, again, which is noisy.

TABLE 2. Measure of Timing Skill (January 1977 to December 1988)

	Merton Score	*Confidence (%)*
British Pound	1.31	99
West German Mark	1.21	99
Japanese Yen	1.09	87
Swiss Franc	1.21	99
French Franc	1.24	99

Source: Windham Capital Management

One might be able to argue that this strategy works more often than not, but perhaps it only works by a marginal amount, and when it fails, it fails by a big amount, so you do not end up making any money. This can be tested. The strategy that I have tested is to assume that I have an underlying investment in Treasury bills and that I can buy or sell currency futures or forward contracts in an amount not greater than 50 percent or not less than -50 percent of my underlying portfolio. **Figures 7 through 11** show the average monthly return of the currency and the average monthly exposure of that strategy for each of the five major currencies. You can see that the strategy is long when the currency's return is positive, and short when the currency's return is negative. Although the currencies are not necessarily highly correlated during this period, the strategy works for all of the currencies.

Figure 12 shows the cumulative wealth line for this strategy versus the benchmark. This is not a very risky strategy because the portfolio is constrained to be no more exposed than plus or minus 50 percent of the underlying T-bill portfolio. The strategy returned 12.3 percent per year, versus 8.66 percent for T-bills, which is almost 4 percent a year for the past 12 years. That 4 percent would apply to any underlying portfolio. If it were applied to an EAFE index fund, you would get 4 percent more than what the EAFE index fund returned. It does not matter

FIGURE 7. British Pound

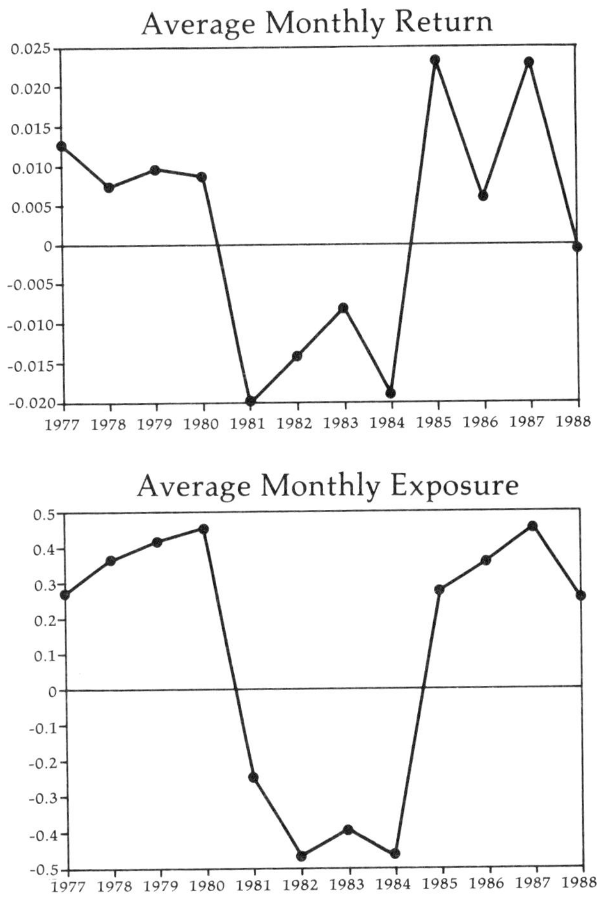

Source: Windham Capital Management

FIGURE 8. West German Mark

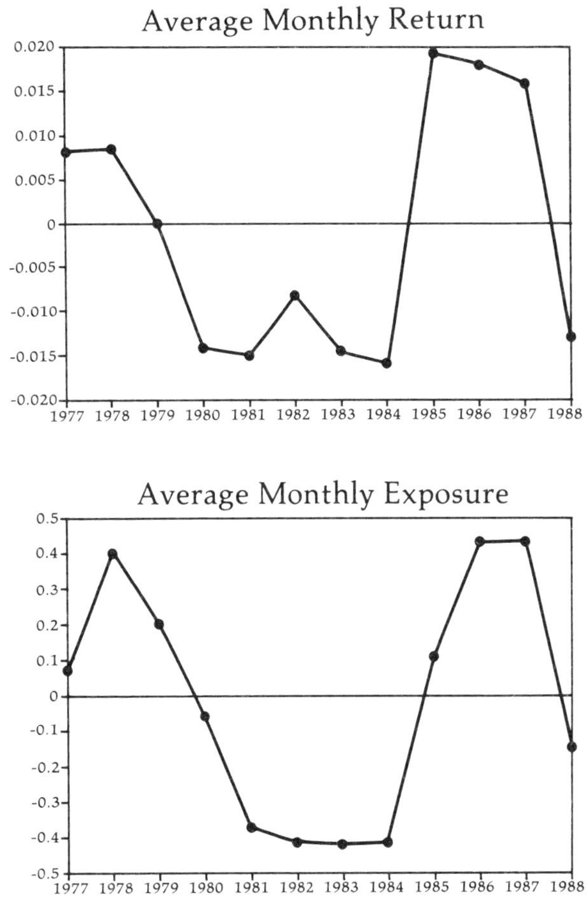

Source: Windham Capital Management

FIGURE 9. Japanese Yen

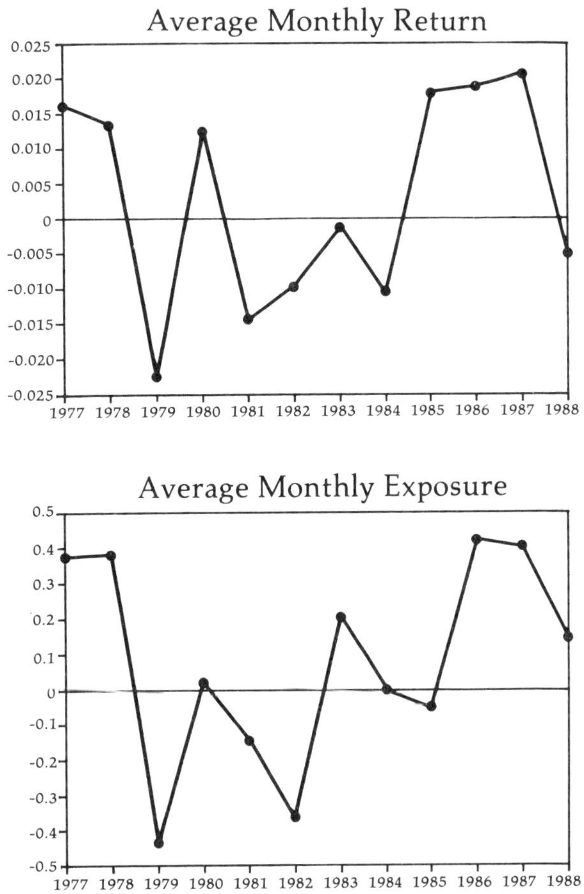

Source: Windham Capital Management

FIGURE 10. Swiss Franc

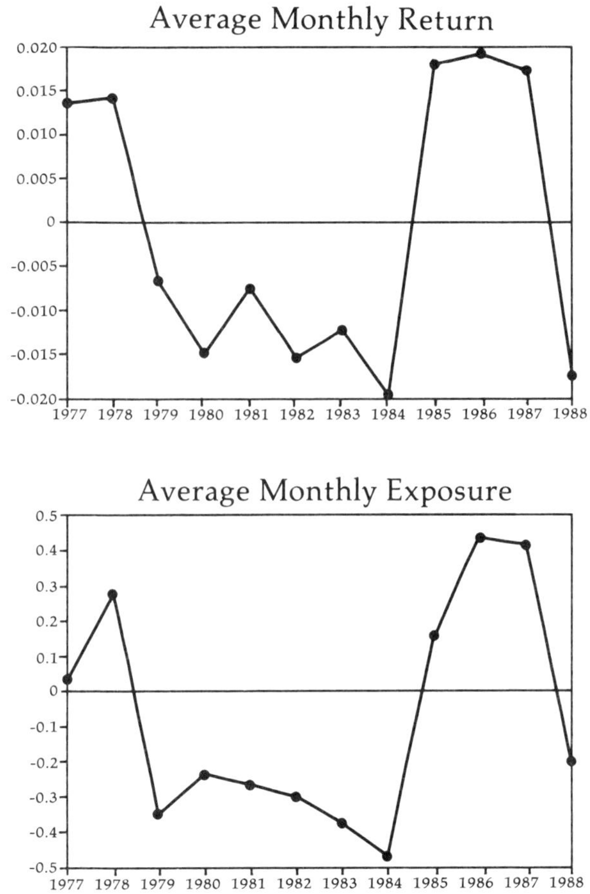

Source: Windham Capital Management

FIGURE 11. French Franc

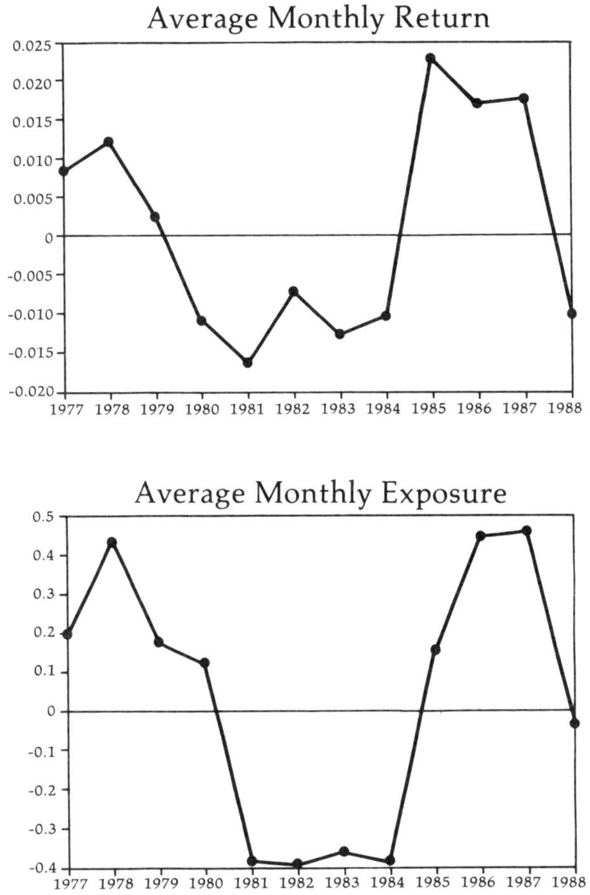

Source: Windham Capital Management

FIGURE 12. Cumulative Wealth

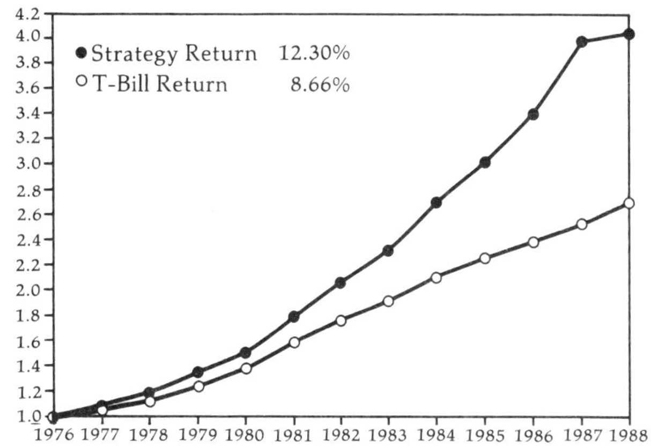

Source: Windham Capital Management

what the underlying portfolio is. The strategy has never had a negative calendar-year return for any of the currencies since 1977, and it has added value in 10.5 out of 12.5 periods.

CONCLUSION

It is my view that central banks induce nonrandomness and they can do this for a long time. It is a cost of promoting stability. There is persuasive evidence of this nonrandomness. There is persuasive evidence of skill in the implicit market-timing signal, and there are strategies that can take advantage of this nonrandomness and make money.

Question and Answer Session

QUESTION: What is the time interval in which the estimate was conducted?

KRITZMAN: The simulation used monthly observations, so it assumed that I revised the portfolio once a month, based strictly on the past month's currency return.

QUESTION: Would you use one month as the trading rule?

KRITZMAN: In actually managing this strategy in real time, I recommend that revisions be based on the magnitude of the currency return from the last time you rebalanced your portfolio, rather than on the passage of time.

QUESTION: What is the magnitude of the serial correlation?

KRITZMAN: I do not know the actual number. It is highly statistically significant.

QUESTION: Has there been any noticeable change in the serial correlation over identifiable periods of history?

KRITZMAN: It has worked over the entire period that I studied and over almost every subperiod. It works whether the dollar goes up or down versus the other currencies. This strategy does not depend on which direction the currency moves; it just matters that it diverts from some equilibrium value.

QUESTION: How important is the normality assumption for the variance ratio test?

KRITZMAN: I do not know, but the fact that there is nonrandomness in the data implies that currency returns are not normal.

QUESTION: Have you done this kind of work for other currencies?

KRITZMAN: The phenomenon results from all the activities of all the central banks. Clearly, the dollar is the most important, and the Federal Reserve is the most important central bank. I have recently tested the strategy with the Australian dollar, and it works quite well there as well. I have not tested the strategy in terms of switching between two non-U.S. currencies. My presumption is that the strategy will work when there is not a lot of covariance between the currencies. So it will not work very well, for example, between the Swiss franc and the West German mark, but it probably will work quite well between the Swiss franc and the Japanese yen.

Evaluating Currencies as a Separate Asset Class

Mack Ott[1]

The first step in evaluating currencies as a separate asset class is to establish whether there is a risk premium. If there is a risk premium, then there is a rate of return to speculative investment; however, there cannot be a risk premium if currencies continuously conform to purchasing power parity—in other words, if the exchange rates are such that one can buy the same goods at a price regardless of currency. If there is a risk premium, then either there must be short-term deviations from purchasing power parity that are systematic in terms of market fundamentals or there must be some inefficiency in the market. In this presentation, I want to give some credibility to the idea that there is a risk premium in efficient exchange markets.

My point of view is premised on the assumption that markets are rational, that people make decisions based on attempting to maximize their own well-being, and that the exchange market has an underlying tendency to return each exchange rate to its fundamentals, i.e., purchasing power parity holds. Later, I will distinguish between rational markets and profit maximization in a pure or narrow sense.

RISK PREMIUM

A risk premium is the extra yield (premium) for bearing uncertainty. It results from the distinction between maximizing wealth, or maximizing the expected value of a portfolio, and maximizing utility. It depends on the concavity of the objective function or, equivalently, diminishing marginal utility. More is better than less, but at a diminishing rate. There are three sources of uncertainty: the real return on the foreign security or investment project, the rate of inflation, and unexpected exchange restrictions or other policy shifts.

Figure 1 shows the utility of wealth with no uncertainty. The utility is the value of the objective function $U(W_1)$. Notice that the function is concave. More wealth is preferred to less, but each increment of wealth adds a smaller amount of utility than the preceding one.

Figure 2 illustrates the expected utility of wealth for a portfolio where there is a range of possible outcomes. In this case, we have a simple bet: either the outcome will be a loss of b resulting in wealth of (W - b) or it will be an increase of b resulting in wealth of (W + b). Notice that the valuation of $E[U(W_1)]$ is smaller than $U[W_1]$. In Figure 2, because the outcome is uncertain—there will either be a loss or a gain—the certainty equivalent, W_2, is lower than $E(W_2)$. People would obtain the same level of utility from W_2 as from the risky contract for W_{1-b} or W_{2+b}. The difference between the expected value and the certainty equivalent is called the risk premium.

There are two ways to hedge the risk: sell the risky contract for its certainty equivalent by sacrificing that yield (the risk premium), or diversify by taking a number of uncorrelated risky bets. **Figure 3** shows the expected utility of wealth with a diversified position. Diversification results in two bets instead of one. In the first case, we had a bet that the portfolio would be either W + b or W - b. With diversification, there are two bets, each of which has a 1/2b or a -1/2b payoff. The two bets are independent; their correlation is zero. The risk premium for the diversified portfolio is significantly less than the risk premium for the undiversified portfolio.

Foreign exchange risk premia also reflect the uncertainty about the term to maturity. Comparing an asset class in two different currencies, the longer the term to maturity, the larger the risk premium on the asset. For example, there will be a smaller risk premium in a three-month Treasury-bill rate compared between the United States and West Germany than there will be in a long-term government bond rate.

PURCHASING POWER PARITY

The existence of a risk premium depends on departures from purchasing power parity. The question is, why does purchasing power parity fail? Why aren't currencies evaluated at a price that would buy the same basket of goods and services

[1]The views and interpretations advanced in this presentation are those of the author and do not necessarily reflect the policy positions of the Federal Reserve Bank of St. Louis.

FIGURE 1. **Utility of Wealth, No Uncertainty**

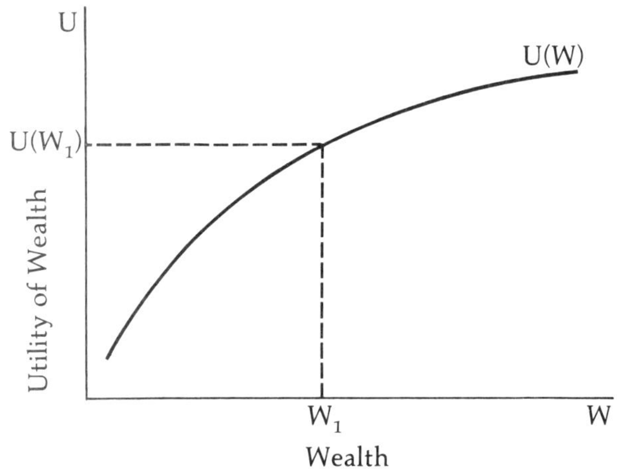

Source: Mack Ott

regardless of the currency? There are three reasons. First, there may be short-run deviations because price adjustments are not instantaneous—information is costly, sellers do not want to change their list prices, and price changes upset buyers. Sticky adjustments in prices can explain a good deal why a currency may or may not be equal to its long-term, fundamental value.

Second, purchasing power parity is a function of relative price changes. The theory of purchasing power parity is not the law of one price. A Toyota should not sell for the same price in San Francisco and in Tokyo, but the price should differ only by transportation costs. It is hard to compare prices because there are factors in a price that are not traded. The British financial weekly *The Economist* publishes the Big Mac Index, an index of the prices of hamburgers in different currencies converted at market exchange rates to dollar prices. Based on that index, they claim that the yen is overvalued relative to the dollar or the pound. In reality, that index represents more than a hamburger, it also represents services—for example, the salaries of the people behind the counter and the taxes on the land, which clearly are more expensive in Tokyo than in Missoula, Montana. So if we talk about an entire package of goods, we are talking about something a lot more complex than simply the price of a single good.

Third, purchasing power parity is a function of expected government policy. What is a government likely to do over the holding period of an asset? The stance of a government and the expected range of policies that a government may implement are important factors in the determination of risk premia

FIGURE 2. Expected Utility of Wealth, The Cost of Uncertainty: Risk Premium

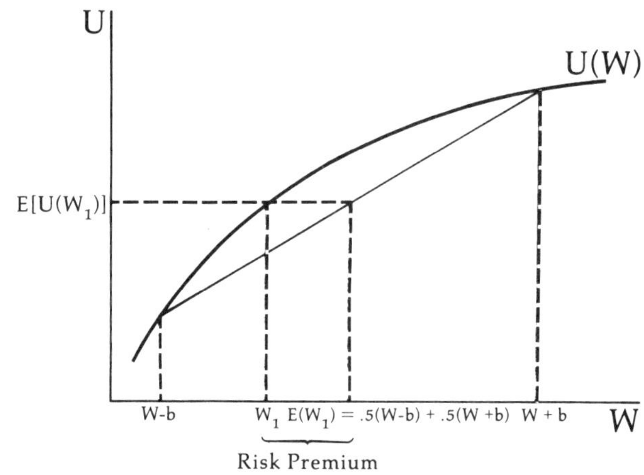

Source: Mack Ott

for holding a particular currency relative to another. People who bought French bonds prior to the election in 1978 were probably disappointed in the performance of their portfolios when the election results became known.

EVALUATING A CURRENCY

There are two ways to evaluate a currency in terms of its movement over time and interest-rate differences: covered interest parity and uncovered interest

FIGURE 3. Expected Utility of Wealth, Diversified: Reduced Risk Premium

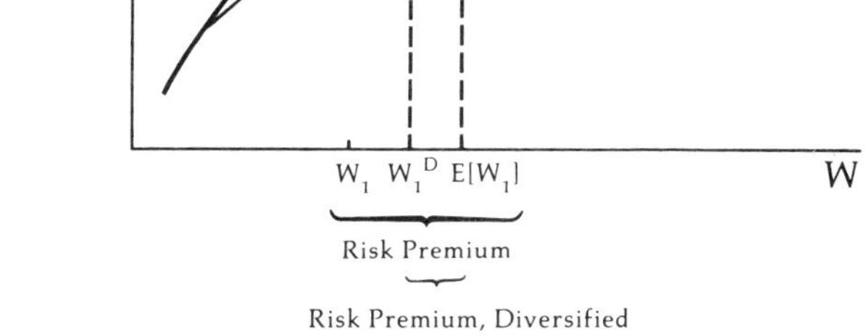

Source: Mack Ott

parity. Covered interest parity is simply the difference between the log of the forward exchange rate and the spot exchange rate, which will be equal to the interest difference, adjusted for differences in timing. For example, the three-month forward premium will be one-fourth of the interest difference, because it is a three-month asset and interest rates are expressed in annual terms.

Some people argue that forward rates are a very poor predictor of future spot rates. Does that tell us that the market is inefficient? No. The forward premium is simply an arbitrage relation. Prior to the organization and development of forward markets, if an investor had wanted to buy currency forward, he would tell his banker the currency he wanted to buy and delivery time. The banker would in turn look at the latest quotes on short-term interest rates over the period that he wanted delivery. The quote would be the spot rate plus a percentage adjustment equal to the interest difference. That is simply an arbitrage relation; it is not a prediction of the future spot rate. If there is an interest premium for the greater riskiness of one currency or another, that premium is going to be different than the point estimate of the future expected spot rate would be. **Exhibit 1** shows the formula for covered interest parity.

Uncovered interest parity is a bit more general, but that generality is bought at the price of containing two variables that are not directly observable, namely the expected future spot rate and the risk premium, P_t. The expected future spot rate must be based upon current information. It is the interest difference between the expected but unobservable future spot rate and the current spot rate, annualized *if* the premium, P_t, is zero. If there is a risk premium, what the market implicitly expects the spot exchange rate to do over the holding period will not be equal to the interest difference. Exhibit 1 also shows the formula for uncovered interest parity.

EXHIBIT 1. Interest Parity Formulas

Covered Interest Parity (CIP):

$$[F_{t+3}-S_t] = (i_3-i_3^*)/4$$

where:

F_{t+3}	=	Log of 3-month forward exchange rate at time t, \$/foreign currency unit.
S_t	=	Log of spot exchange rate at time t.
i_3	=	U.S. interest rate on 3-month securities.
i_3^*	=	foreign interest rate on 3-month securities.

Uncovered Interest Parity (UIP):

$$4\{E[S_{t+3} \mid I_t] - S_t\} + P_{t+3} = i_3-i_3^*$$

where:

$E_t[S_{t+3} \mid I_t]$	=	Expected log of spot exchange rate 3 months hence given market information (I_t) at time t.
P_{t+3}	=	Risk premium in interest units on 3-month securities.

There is substantial empirical evidence that there is a risk premium. There is evidence both in foreign exchange rates and domestic interest rates such as Treasury-bill yields that individuals make decisions in a risk-averse way, requiring an extra premium for taking on a risky outcome.

If the market is efficient, the expected future spot exchange rate can be solved for using the uncovered parity relation. This is in the spirit of the modern theory of exchange rates, which treats monies simply as a particular kind of asset. The current spot rate is simply the discounted value of the expected future spot rate, with the discount factor equal to the risk-adjusted interest differential ($i-i^*-P_t$). **Exhibit 2** shows how the current spot exchange rate depends on expectations and the risk premium.

The risk premium increases with the length of the term to maturity of the asset. In the uncovered interest parity equation, αj is the annualizing factor, one-fourth for a three-month contract and 30 for a 30-year contract. That means that a given change in interest differentials on long instruments has a much greater impact on the current spot rate, adjusted for anticipated future movements, than does an equal change in the short rate differential.

If the market adjusts only with respect to purchasing power parity, then one would expect the dollar price of the yen to rise at a rate equal to the difference between the expected U.S. inflation rate and the Japanese inflation rate. That would maintain purchasing power parity. To predict future spot rates requires a prediction about what the future inflation rate will be. If the anticipated inflation rate in the United States goes down, then over time the purchasing power parity exchange rate will also go down. It will go down by an amount that reflects the change in the anticipated inflation rate over the holding period.

THE CHALLENGES OF INVESTING IN FOREIGN CURRENCIES

Suppose that the U.S. government lowers taxes on investment projects. The immediate impact of that is

EXHIBIT 2. Implied Spot Rate Relation

UIP (Uncovered Interest Parity):

$$\frac{1}{\alpha_j}\{E[S_{t+j} \mid I_t] - S_t\} + P_{t+j} = i_j-i_j^*$$

$$\alpha_j = \begin{cases} 1/4 \text{ for } j = 3 \text{ Months} \\ 30 \text{ for } j = 30 \text{ Years} \end{cases}$$

Implied Spot Rate Relation:

$$S_t = E[S_{t+j} \mid I_t] - \alpha_j[P_{t+j} - (i_j-i_j^*)]$$

to raise the after-tax rate of return on U.S. assets, which attracts capital from other parts of the world to the United States, bidding up the price of the dollar. The investor's challenge is to determine how long the adjustment process will take—how long it will take to bring the rate of return in the United States at purchasing power parity back to what it was prior to the change. **Figure 4** illustrates how the speed of exchange-rate adjustments affects speculative yield. If the adjustment process takes a long time, then the time at which purchasing power parity will be restored will also be farther out along the time axis. The longer the adjustment process, the greater the opportunity to profit from speculating against the foreign currency.

Suppose the central bank resists movements in the exchange rate that are going to take place eventually. If the investor has a longer horizon than the central bank, he can make money by buying the currency when the central bank is selling it, and selling the currency when the central bank is buying it. If the monetary authorities' policy is correctly anticipated and the investor is willing to wait, he will make money. It is possible to do that, not only in foreign exchange markets but also in domestic markets, because the U.S. monetary authorities (i.e., the Fed and the Treasury) typically sterilize a large portion of what they do in intervention. So if they are selling dollars, they will be taking them out of the domestic market by selling T-bills. They will be trying to keep the dollar from rising, but to keep domestic monetary policy on track, they will also be taking reserves out of the domestic market. This will

FIGURE 4. Speed of Exchange-Rate Adjustment Affects Speculative Yield

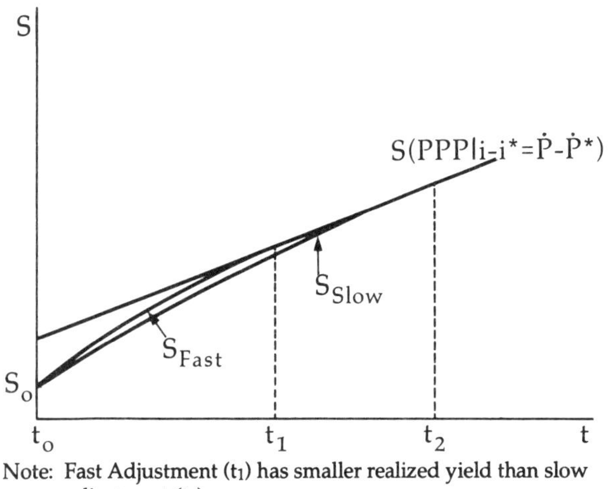

Note: Fast Adjustment (t_1) has smaller realized yield than slow adjustment (t_2).

Source: Mack Ott

drive up interest rates and drive down bond prices. So money can be made by betting against the central bank, either internationally or domestically, as long as the central bank is opposing exchange-rate movements caused by fundamentals.

It is not possible to make money speculating on currencies unless there is a risk premium, because if there is not, then purchasing power parity would hold exactly. We have to know something about the timing of the adjustment, or what the central bank is going to do, or how long a particular irrational policy is going to be engaged in.

EVIDENCE IN SUPPORT OF RISK PREMIA IN FOREIGN EXCHANGE RATES

Two recent articles support the assertion that there are risk premia present in foreign exchange rates. The first is by Eugene Fama (1984). Fama's research has been replicated and tinkered with by a host of talented economists and mathematical statisticians at Carnegie Mellon, Chicago, and Rochester. All find basically the same result: There is a time-varying risk premium in forward exchange rates that is revealed in the variance of the spot forward exchange rate, in terms of the forward premium.

The other evidence in support of risk premia is from a very different standpoint—the survey data of foreign exchange traders' expectations. Frankel and Froot (1987) found evidence of a risk premium in spot forecasts of future exchange rates gathered by money market services, AMEX, and *The Economist*—three different sets of surveys. This finding has been replicated using British data as well as the U.S. data. It is statistically significant, but it does not fully account for the forward-rate bias.

The risk premium does not have to be an irrational bias; it can result from real shocks, or it can result from slow-to-adjust prices. The key to decision-making about currency speculation is the expected exchange rate. This expectation depends both on fundamentals and political economy aspects—issues such as whether the United Kingdom will join the EMS joint float.

The options market is an indirect way of approaching it. Take a speculative position and compute the extra rate of return that separates it from a fully hedged position. The implied loss if the expectation is wrong can be limited by buying an option that is sufficiently out of the money. However, an interesting characteristic of option prices is that the farther out of the money option prices are, the more they tend to be overpriced. That is, in a sense, a refutation of very simple models of option pricing. Consequently, if they are rationally determined, these prices must be distributed in some way other than normally. I believe this attribute reflects the fact that as the strike price gets farther away from the current spot, even though its likelihood is diminishing very rapidly, people become more and more concerned about the implications of what this unlikely event would mean for their wealth. This is what we looked at in the concave function of Figure 1.

CONCLUSION

The key to decision-making about currency speculation and hedge ratios is to implicitly make an estimate of what the future spot exchange rate will be. For this purpose, both the options market and outguessing the central bank are ingredients in a speculative strategy. If markets are stable and, in the long-run, spot exchange rates follow fundamentals, then there is a very strong case to be made for a risk premium embodied in currencies that is neither trivial nor irrational. It is the payment for a real cost—the cost of bearing uncertainty.

Question and Answer Session

QUESTION: How can practitioners benefit from being able to anticipate what central bankers are doing?

OTT: If you believe that exchange rates deviate from market fundamentals because of a set of stable or basically predictable relationships, then your long-run prediction about the exchange rate determines the extent to which you are going to speculate. You need to know why the central bank is intervening. Recently, the central banks—not just the United States, but all central banks—have intervened because the dollar is too high. If the dollar is increasing in value, and the central bank is selling dollars, they are performing something that a private, profit-making entity would not do. The Fed does it because it prints the money. It is very simple; it does not cost the Fed anything. A company would not do it.

One investment strategy is to be on the other side of the Fed. Central banks intervene because the currency is moving in a direction they do not want it to move in. But if you believe that currency movements are based on fundamentals, the currency movement is correct. In that scenario, even if the central bank does not like it, the currency is eventually going to go in that direction anyway. Therefore, as long as your holding period for the currency is longer than the central bank's, you will make money.

QUESTION: How is this model a factor in the unanticipated shifts in inflation expectations in a country's economy?

OTT: The first step is to predict exchange rates. By definition, a risk premium bears uncertainty. Information is not fully incorporated in prices, in part because the adjustment process is slow or the guesses that people are making are not close enough to certainty equivalents. If there is new information that is opposite to your guess, then you are going to lose. When you take a position that is bullish on the dollar you are making an implicit statement. For example, you are saying the Saudis are going to continue to produce 4 to 6 billion barrels a day rather than 2 million barrels a day. Those types of assumptions are implicit, including that you have the right estimate of the inflation rates.

QUESTION: Who pays the risk premium? Can both sides of the exchange rate be simultaneously compensated for bearing risk?

OTT: The simple answer is that a risk premium reflects a relative uncertainty of one currency versus another. So the risk premium is always in one direction at any particular time. Currently, the United States has a large risk against the Japanese yen, because interest differentials are higher than the inflation difference between the United States and Japan. That risk premium against the dollar is negative against the British pound.

QUESTION: At what point does it become too expensive for central banks to intervene?

OTT: The answer depends on the central bank's policy goal. For example, in Switzerland, the rule is that the Swiss franc should sell for about 1.2 West German marks. The reason is that such a large portion of Swiss trade is with West Germany, and West German monetary policy has been relatively stable in the past couple of decades. The Swiss have accepted that sort of shadow process of pegging the rate. On the other hand, suppose that the West German central bank decided they wanted to get rid of all the Greens in Parliament. Suppose monetary growth ran to 20 percent a year instead of the 9 to 10 percent that it has over the past couple of years. At some point, the Swiss franc would start appreciating versus the mark, and they would have to decide whether they wanted to maintain parity and a nominal basis with West Germany, at the risk of long-run inflation and losing credibility on monetary policy, or to let the franc appreciate versus the mark.

QUESTION: Do you think it is possible to anticipate what is going to be happening in the foreign exchange markets and to be able to structure portfolios that make currency decisions at the same time as asset decisions? Or, should one hedge the risk?

OTT: The 77 percent hedge rate that Fischer Black advocated in his presentation was based upon a fairly strict set of assumptions.[1] If purchasing power

[1]See Mr. Black's presentation, pp. 28-32.

parity is holding continuously, as it was in Black's model, and if everybody has the same information, then Fischer Black's prescription is to diversify. You not only hold a diversified domestic portfolio, but you hold a portfolio of foreign assets, and then you diversify one step further—you hold it in foreign currency. So you take advantage of the less-than-perfect correlation of currency movements and asset prices. Black is saying that by diversifying, you are getting the advantage that would result in whatever residual non-perfect correlation there was between assets in that world. But it is difficult to see that there would be any such different movement.

On the other hand, you could speculate. To make a prediction about where exchange rates are going to go, either you must believe that your information is better than everyone else's or you must be prepared to take the risk associated with the risk premium. If the central bank behaves in an iteratively revealed and irrational way, you can make money using that information. On the other hand, if there is greater variability of one asset group versus another, in a rational market you would expect to be rewarded with a higher rate of return. Neither of those things is inconsistent with either rational or efficient markets.

Beyond these arguments, there seems to be a strange persistence in price changes. I have found evidence of that persistence in a balanced portfolio model, where lagged exchange-rate changes for each of the G7 currencies versus the dollar have significant *t*-statistics, using quarterly data. That is difficult to rationalize. One might expect it over a week or a month or a day, but over a quarter it is strange. That seems to be a sticky market or a kind of an inefficiency. Thus, I would argue against hedging the entire portfolio.

Using Derivatives to Execute Currency Strategies

Dean D'Onofrio, CFA

Most of the presentations in these proceedings have been devoted to discussions of various currency management policies. Once a currency strategy has been decided upon, the investor is then faced with choosing among alternative methods of execution. I will discuss the use of derivative securities to execute currency strategies.

The main considerations in choosing the appropriate instruments are liquidity, cash flow dynamics, proxy basket selection, and maturity. In considering the available instruments, it is important to realize that the foreign exchange market exists, primarily, as a means of hedging known cash flows. Hedging the value of a portfolio of assets is a relatively recent phenomenon.

Three basic instruments are available for bilateral foreign exchange transactions: futures, forward contracts, and options. The volume in currency derivative security transactions is quite large. For example, in 1988 the yen futures volume alone exceeded $500 billion on the Chicago Mercantile Exchange. Although huge, as **Table 1** shows, the futures market is really the poor cousin of the forward market in terms of volume of transactions.

FUTURES MARKET

The objective of the hedge will determine how long or short a position in the instrument one should take, and what the composition of that position should be. Using futures to hedge cash flows can be inflexible, however, because the size of contracts and maturities of the contracts are fixed. Nonetheless, futures are used effectively to hedge portfolios, particularly small ones.

The most talked-about idiosyncrasy of hedging is probably cash-flow dynamics. Because futures are marked to market daily, they require an ability to raise or receive cash daily. Raising cash is not always easy. It can be very expensive to liquidate portions of an equity portfolio, particularly international equities, to raise cash. In addition, holding a pool of cash in lieu of equities represents a significant opportunity cost. To help alleviate this problem, we recommend the use of stock index futures as a substitute for a fraction of one's equity exposure.

Futures contracts do have several attractive features. First, credit risk is not as big a factor as with a forward contract. Credit risk was a bit overlooked before the crash; now it is very much in the front of everyone's mind when we talk about derivative securities. The risk of not being paid on a futures contract is limited to one day's movement because accounts are marked to market on a daily basis. Investors should be aware, however, that the credit risk of a futures transaction is heavily influenced by the balance in the book of business of the futures clearing merchant that you are dealing with.

Second, the futures market creates a central pricing mechanism. This is probably the biggest economic benefit of futures. All market participants can get a quote of the last execution. This information allows arbitrage to keep the forward and the futures markets in line more easily.

Finally, futures contracts are traded with a central clearing mechanism. This allows positions to be placed and removed, rather than merely offset.

FORWARD CONTRACTS

There are several advantages to using forward contracts. First, forward contracts can be put on in virtually any currency, in virtually any size, and for virtually any maturity. This makes them the instrument of choice for most cash-flow hedgers. Until recently, cash-flow hedgers completely dominated this industry. Cash-flow hedgers are institutions that are interested in hedging flows of funds—commercial banks and international corporations, for example. Unlike futures contracts, these instruments are settled at maturity. Also, unlike futures contracts, currency must be delivered as stipulated in the contract. Trades can be settled in dollars by trading in the spot market. But, because transactions must be arranged at least two days in advance, this so-called spot market is really a two-day forward market for many currencies.

The credit risk of this market is also different than that of the futures market. There is no initial margin posted, and the total amount of profit or loss

TABLE 1. Buying and Selling Currency Forward Using Futures Contracts

Contract	1988 Volume (Thousands of Contracts)	Contract Size	Current U.S. $ Value of One Contract ($000)
Japanese Yen	6,433.1	12.5 MM Yen	$86.3
Deutsche Mark	5,662.1	125,000 Marks	63.2
Swiss Frank	5,283.4	125,000 Francs	73.2
British Pound Sterling	2,616.1	62,500 Pounds	96.4
Canadian Dollar	1,408.8	100,000 Dollars	83.4
Australian Dollar	76.0	100,000 Dollars	75.4

Source: Bankers Trust Company

is due at expiration. Consequently, the size of each payment will be much greater when using forward contracts because they are not settled on a daily profit-and-loss basis.

Clearing is one of the biggest disadvantages of the forward market. There is no central clearing. Therefore, an investor must have a good back office to trade forward contracts at low administrative costs.

Finally, the pricing of forward contracts is a bit more variant than in the futures market, because there exists the possibility that you can be an uninformed market participant. Arbitrage does occur between the futures market and the forward market, but unless you are aware of where the market really is, you can be quoted unattractive prices.

Table 2 provides estimates of typical transaction costs expected in the forward market. There are no commissions; this is purely a dealer's spread market. The table is organized into groups according to the liquidity of the contract. The most liquid contract is yen-dollar. The cheapest trade on that contract is likely to be about three basis points—that is, the total bid-ask spread as a percentage of the mean of the then-current bid-ask spot spread. For the most liquid currencies, the spread seems to double, and for the least liquid, the spread seems to triple when moving from one month to twelve months.

TABLE 2. Transaction Costs in the Forward Market

	1-Month*	12-Month
Yen	0.0003%	2.0x
Deutsche Mark	0.0003%	2.0x
Sterling	0.0003%	2.0x
Swiss Franc	0.0003%	2.0x
French Franc	0.0005%	2.5x
Guilder	0.0005%	2.5x
Lira	0.0005%	2.5x
Remaining European Monetary System	0.0005%	2.5x
Australian Dollar	0.0005%	2.5x
Singapore Dollar	0.0005%	2.5x
New Zealand Dollar	0.0015%	3.0x

* Expected bid-ask spread as a percentage of spot rate.

Source: Bankers Trust Company

It appears that it would be relatively inexpensive in terms of transaction costs to hedge a fixed dollar amount forward for a year. However, if you do not know how much actual equity value you are going to have a year from now and your intent is to replicate the return of a fully hedged portfolio—e.g., the local market index—then you are going to have to reset your hedges on a much more frequent basis, and pay the shorter-term transaction costs. So, as usual in the index replication game, investors are confronted with a trade-off between the known drag of transaction costs and the potential randomness of not exactly replicating the index.

Figure 1 shows what actually happens when you sell the yen forward, in terms of the cash flow that will either accrue to the portfolio or will be owed by the portfolio, as a result of the change in the spot rate at the time of expiration. The yen currently trades at a forward premium because interest rates are lower in Japan than they are in the United States. Therefore, if the spot rate at expiration ($spot_1$) is equal to the spot rate today ($spot_0$), you would earn a positive rate of return equal to the intersection of the forward line with the y axis. In fact, you will earn a positive rate of return, or positive cash flow, from putting on this yen hedge, as long as the yen does not appreciate by an amount greater than that implied in

FIGURE 1. Hedging Currencies Priced at Forward Premiums

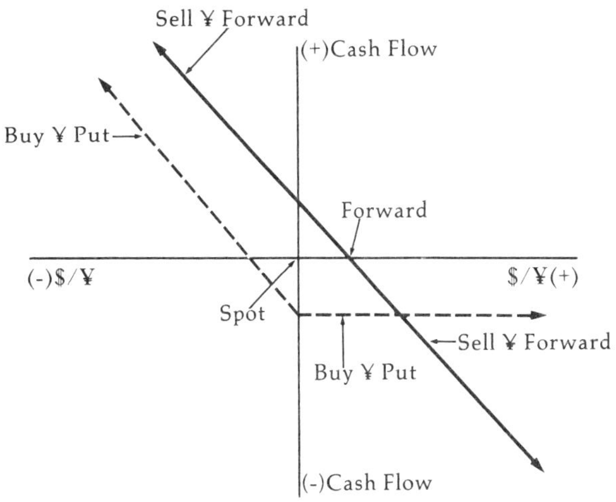

Source: Bankers Trust Company

the forward rate.

Figure 1 also shows the cost of a put on the yen. It represents the cost of a put going out about three months, with the strike price equal to today's spot. The cost of that put is about 1.75 percent of the total market value of the portfolio. In other words, if I had enough yen to cover today's spot rate and I had enough money to buy the put, the cost of the put as a percentage of my total wealth would be 1.75 percent.

This percentage is not the same for currencies that are priced at a forward discount. **Figure 2** shows the return distribution of selling pounds forward and buying a put on pounds. Essentially, we see the reverse of what occurred with the yen. If you sold pounds forward and the pound spot rate declined, it would still be possible to lose money on the transaction. To earn a positive cash flow on this transaction, the pound rate has to drop by an amount greater than that implied in the forward rate. Pricing a put option on the pound with a strike price equal to today's spot rate reveals the cost going up to almost 3 percent, as opposed to less than 2 percent for the yen. This essentially reflects the difference in the two forward rate curves. However, if I priced the two options with the strike price equal to the forward rate, the price of the options as a percentage of total wealth are both priced around 2.25 percent. Therefore, 2.25 percent appears to be the price that reflects the market's perception of spot volatility or uncertainty. The difference between 2.25 percent and the actual price may be interpreted as the price one pays as a result of the forward premium or discount.

FIGURE 2. Hedging Currencies Priced at Forward Discounts

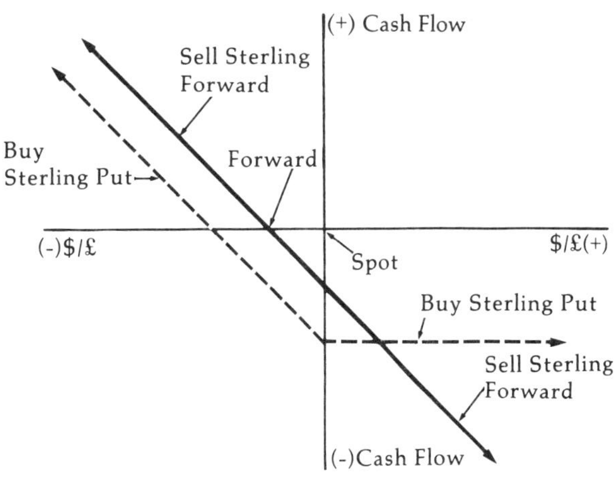

Source: Bankers Trust Company

OPTIONS

The third instrument available is an option. When discussing options, investors should be aware that simple options are by no means the only choice available for skewing the expected return patterns. In fact, a simple put option implies an infinite disutility for earnings rate below that implied by the strike price. I do not imagine this utility function is very common among institutional investors.

Option strategies, however, may be structured to meet an investor's actual utility function. This is the benefit of the over-the-counter options market. Options have been created on the actual dollar value of foreign assets, which is what most investors are concerned with. There are options on the value of baskets of currencies, as opposed to individual currencies or options on the dollar value of baskets of foreign assets. One of the more popular types of options is the so-called path-dependent option, where, depending upon the path of prices between now and expiration, the option either explodes or comes into play.

THE COST OF HEDGING

The cost of executing a hedge is a primary concern among investors. It is difficult to predict expected costs, however, because costs will be highly dependent upon just how far forward you sell, whether you merely sell forward or whether you demand some type of skewness—i.e., use an option—and how often you roll. One must also consider the costs above and beyond transaction costs. To execute a hedge, you are performing a transaction for which you must pay some type of dealer spread in exchange for the liquidity you are demanding. In addition, if the market perceives that you are receiving a risk-reduction benefit from hedging, you should expect to pay a price for that benefit (unless you believe markets are inefficient). This is one reason why options are generally more expensive than just selling forward; options provide the benefit of skewness.

It is possible that when you execute a forward trade in the foreign exchange market, you may be purchasing a risk-reduction benefit and thereby asking someone else to provide that benefit to you. If there is no risk-reduction benefit or cost to hedging beyond transaction costs, then in the long run spot rates would move to forward rates, because that is the only condition in which there is no net cash flow created by the forward transaction. Therefore, if there is no risk premium, there is no cost to hedging other than paying a dealer in the middle.

If you believe there is a risk premium, then the

FIGURE 3. Implication of Random Walk Hypothesis

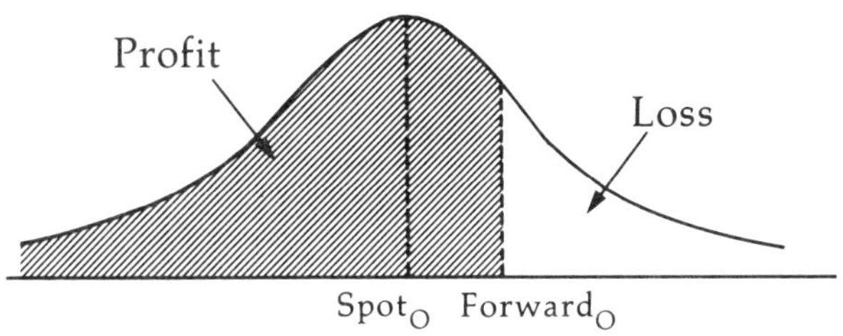

Source: Bankers Trust Company

FIGURE 4. Distribution of Expected Outcomes: Spot$_T$

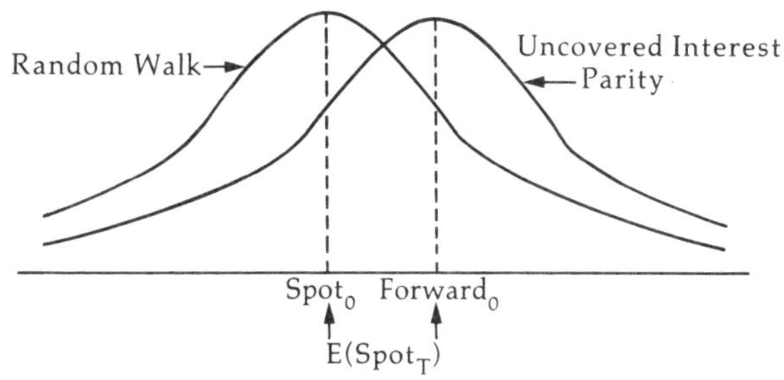

Source: Bankers Trust Company

price at which forward trades occur—i.e., the forward rate—will reflect the premium; the trader accepting risk receives a payment and the trader reducing risk makes a payment.

Figure 3 shows an extreme view of the so-called random walk hypothesis. By random walk, I mean that the current spot is considered to be the best predictor of the future spot rate. **Figure 4** shows the distribution of expected outcomes for two risk premium assumptions: the random walk and the "uncovered interest parity" hypothesis, which is where the risk premium equals zero.

If one believes there are risk premiums associated with forward exchanges—i.e., the expected spot is different than the forward rate you observe today—then there will be either some cost or some benefit to hedging, depending upon which side of the risk reduction equation you are on. If the random walk hypothesis holds, someone who is hedging a position in yen back to dollars, i.e., selling forward yen into dollars, is doing so at a negative expected cost or actually a positive net cash flow. Hence, even though that person is going to incur transaction costs because the net risk-reduction benefit that he provides to the party on the other side of the trade is not an insignificant amount, he is trading with a positive expected return.

CONCLUSION

If you believe the best predictor of where the spot rate is going to be in the future is something other than the forward rate, then you can justify managing currency exposure as a separate asset class. If you believe that the spot rate is going to move to the forward rate on average, then you are wasting your time trying to manage currencies, and a fully hedged position is suggested. Regardless of your convictions about the existence of risk premiums, however, it is extremely unlikely that the currency exposures implied by equity holdings are optimal.

Question and Answer Session

QUESTION: Which foreign index futures are approved for U.S. investors by the Commodities Futures Trading Commission?

D'ONOFRIO: To my knowledge, the only foreign index contract is the Nikkei 225, which trades on the SIMEX.

QUESTION: Has any work been done that looks at the hedge decision given the fact that hedging through options has an asymmetric payoff, whereas hedging through forward contracts has a symmetric payoff?

D'ONOFRIO: Hedging with options was very popular a couple of years ago in the United States. The strategy is based on the assumption that investors' risk tolerance is a positive function of their wealth, meaning that as investors become more wealthy, they are willing to take more risk. Therefore, an option-like strategy or a convex strategy makes sense, because owning an option will cause you to be more exposed to the asset as you make money and less exposed to the asset as you start to lose money. Not everyone has the same utility function. For example, referring to my figure which shows the purchase of a listed option, the investor has implicitly stated that he has an infinite disutility to own anything less than the strike price at a certain period of time. This type of utility function may be valid for someone who is saving to put their children through college, but I cannot believe that it is necessarily true for most institutional investors. Consequently, while option-like strategies are very much in demand, simply buying or selling options is probably suboptimal.

Reference List

Black, Fischer. 1989a. "Equilibrium Exchange Rate Hedging." Goldman, Sachs & Co. (Revised April)

__________. 1989b. "Universal Hedging." Goldman, Sachs & Co. (Revised May)

__________. 1974. "International Capital Market Equilibrium with Investment Barriers." *Journal of Financial Economics* (December).

Bostock, Paul, Paul Wooley, and Martin Duffy. 1989. "Duration-Based Asset Allocation." *Financial Analysts Journal* (January/February): 53-60.

Brinson, Gary P. and Roger G. Ibbotson. 1987. *Investment Markets: Gaining the Performance Advantage.* New York: McGraw-Hill, Inc.

Fama, Eugene F. 1984. "Forward and Spot Exchange Rates." *Journal of Monetary Economics* (November): 319-38.

Frankel, Jeffrey A. and Kenneth A. Froot. 1987. "Using Survey Data to Test Standard Propositions Regarding Exchange Rate Expectations." *American Economic Review* (March): 133-53.

Lessard, D. 1976. "World, Country, and Industry Relationships in Equity Returns. *Financial Analysts Journal* (January/February): 32-38.

McEnally, Richard. W., editor. 1986. *International Bonds and Currencies.* Charlottesville, VA: Institute of Chartered Financial Analysts Continuing Education Series.

Merton, Robert. 1981. "On Market Timing and Investment Performance: An Equilibrium Theory of Value for Market Forecasts." *Journal of Business* 54: 3 (363-405).

Perold, André F. and Evan C. Schulman. 1988. "The Free Lunch in Currency Hedging: Implications for Investment Policy and Performance Standards." *Financial Analysts Journal* 44 (May/June): 45-50.

Perold, André F. and William F. Sharpe. 1988. "Dynamic Strategies for Asset Allocation." *Financial Analysts Journal* (January/February): 16-27.

Riehl, Heinz and Rita M. Rodriguez. 1983. *Foreign Exchange and Money Markets.* New York: McGraw-Hill, Inc.

Siegel, Jeremy J. 1972. "Risk, Interest Rates, and the Forward Exchange." *Quarterly Journal of Economics* (May): 303-9.

Solnik, Bruno H. 1988. *International Investments.* Reading, MA: Addison-Wesley.

__________ . 1982. "Optimal International Asset Allocation." *The Journal of Portfolio Management.* (Fall): 11-21.

__________ . 1974. "Why Not Diversify Internationally?" *Financial Analysts Journal* (July/August): 48-54.

__________ . 1973. *European Capital Markets: Towards a General Theory of International Investment.* Lexington Books-D.C. Heath.

Stulz, Rene. 1981. "A Model of International Asset Pricing." *Journal of Financial Economics* 9 (December): 383-406.

Vertin, James R., editor. 1984. *International Equity Investing.* Charlottesville, VA: Institute of Chartered Financial Analysts Continuing Education Series.

Self Evaluation Examination

1. Currency hedging modifies the risk-return characteristics of foreign assets.

   a. True.
   b. False.

2. In terms of currency hedging policy, Rhodes concludes that all of the following are appropriate *except:*

   a. Hedging currency risk is beneficial.
   b. A tactical deviation from a normal currency hedging policy may be appropriate depending on the environment.
   c. Plans with substantial foreign assets should hedge a greater portion of the currency risk than plans with fewer foreign assets.
   d. There is a fixed proportion of every portfolio that should be hedged.

3. According to Proffer, there are several reasons why plan sponsors should hedge, including:

   a. To protect against a weakening U.S. dollar.
   b. To manage volatility.
   c. To capture increased returns by assuming increased risk.
   d. None of the above.

4. In the area of international investment, plan sponsors must make which of the following asset allocation decisions:

   a. The allocation between domestic assets and international assets.
   b. The allocation between international stocks and international bonds.
   c. The allocation between international assets and international currencies.
   d. All of the above.

5. Lee concludes that the application of tactical currency management has value added that may be directly proportional to currency volatility.

   a. True.
   b. False.

6. Lee concludes that the optimal policy level of currency exposure may be zero over the long run.

   a. True.
   b. False.

7. In his presentation, Rosenberg concludes that:

   a. There is a "free lunch" available by passively hedging a foreign portfolio.
   b. Currency hedging is not cost efficient.
   c. Currency hedging should be used as a tactical tool to manage currency risk actively in a global portfolio.
   d. None of the above.

8. Rosenberg concludes that it is largely irrelevant whether one uses a hedged or an unhedged benchmark.

   a. True.
   b. False.

9. The major argument in favor of currency hedging is that:

   a. It increases the return of the portfolio.
   b. It increases the return and the risk of the portfolio.
   c. It lowers the volatility of the portfolio.
   d. It is not expensive to implement.

10. The effectiveness of hedged versus unhedged portfolios is influenced by many considerations, including:

   a. The correlation of assets.
   b. The costs of hedging.
   c. The loss of diversification.
   d. All of the above.

11. Continuous hedging does not affect the diversification of the portfolio.

   a. True.
   b. False.

12. According to Black, all investors should hedge their foreign stocks by the same percentage, and this percentage is always less than 100 percent.

   a. True.
   b. False.

13. Siegel's paradox means that:

   a. Exchange-rate bets are a zero-sum game.
   b. Exchange-rate bets are a negative-sum game.
   c. Exchange-rate bets are a positive-sum game.
   d. Siegel's paradox is merely a mathematical fact that does not apply to exchange-rate bets.

14. Black's formula for the optimal fraction to hedge relies on which of the following variables?

   a. The expected currency changes.
   b. The weighted average risk premium across currencies.
   c. The correlation between currency movements and stock movements.
   d. All of the above.

15. According to Kritzman, there are several considerations that determine the desirability of hedging, including:

   a. The currency's expected return.
   b. The currency's risk.
   c. The currency's hedging effectiveness.
   d. All of the above.

16. According to Kritzman, the optimal hedge ratio depends on:

    a. The equilibrium expected currency changes.
    b. The correlation between the currency and the assets.
    c. The dynamics of the interest-rate differentials.
    d. All of the above.

17. There can be a risk premium in currency markets, according to Ott, if:

    a. Currencies continuously conform to purchasing power parity.
    b. There are short-term deviations from purchasing power parity that are systematic in terms of market fundamentals.
    c. Markets are efficient.
    d. None of the above; there is no risk premium.

18. There are several considerations in choosing the appropriate method of executing a currency management policy, including:

    a. Liquidity.
    b. Cash flow dynamics.
    c. Maturity.
    d. All of the above.

19. According to D'Onofrio, the instrument of choice for most cash-flow hedgers is:

    a. Futures.
    b. Forward contracts.
    c. Options.
    d. Spot market.

20. According to Kritzman, the divergence of opinion voiced by the speakers in these proceedings:

    a. Reflects the fact that people do not understand the problem.
    b. Can be reconciled by noting that the speakers base their analyses on different assumptions.
    c. Cannot be reconciled.
    d. Is a serious issue that must be addressed in a later seminar.

Self-Evaluation Answers

See Rhodes:
1. a True.
2. d Fischer Black argues that there is a fixed proportion; Rhodes does not.

See Proffer:
3. b

See Lee:
4. d
5. a True. This occurs in an environment of a fully hedged, neutral currency position.
6. a True. But, he also concludes that it may be 100 percent.

See Rosenberg:
7. c
8. a Because he concludes the same minimum-risk portfolio will be obtained whether one is hedged or unhedged.

See Carr:
9. c
10. d
11. b False. Continuous hedging does affect diversification because it results in the creation of a synthetic U.S. instrument. Therefore, because of arbitrage in forward exchange markets, yields ought to be the same as for U.S. assets.

See Black:
12. a True.
13. c
14. b

See Kritzman:
15. d
16 b

See Ott:
17. b

See D'Onofrio:
18. d
19. b

See Overview of the Seminar:
20. b